The Pocket Mentor for Game Community Management

Want to work in community management in the games industry? Then this is the book for you. Filled with practical advice and real-world examples, this guide offers a comprehensive introduction to building and nurturing vibrant gaming communities, fostering engagement, and handling challenges along the way.

This book covers everything from the education you'll need, how to look for and apply for job opportunities, and the studio interview process itself. It also includes tips and advice for what to do once you're in the role, with chapters covering strategy, project management, accessibility, and dealing with trolls and toxicity. This book features insights from interviews with dozens of community managers, distilling their expertise into actionable advice. Drawing from recent job listings and seasoned community professionals' experiences, it offers a comprehensive skill set that reflects the dynamic demands of community jobs in the gaming industry.

This book will be of great interest to all beginner and aspiring games community managers.

Carolin Wendt is a professional with more than nine years of games industry experience. She leads a team of international community managers at CD PROJEKT RED. In addition to a strong passion for games and learning about the most obscure things, she's armed with a master's degree in Political Science.

The Pocket Mentors for Games Careers

The Pocket Mentors for Games Careers provides the essential information and guidance needed to get and keep a job in the modern games industry. They explain in simple, clear language exactly what a beginner needs to know about education requirements, finding job opportunities, applying for roles, and acing studio interviews. Readers will learn how to navigate studio hierarchies, transfer roles and companies, work overseas, and develop their skills.

The Pocket Mentor for Video Game Writers
Anna Megill

The Pocket Mentor for Video Game Testing
Harún Ali

The Pocket Mentor for Game Community Management
Carolin Wendt

For more information about this series, please visit: http://www.routledge.com/European-Animation/book-series/PMGC

The Pocket Mentor for Game Community Management

Carolin Wendt

Edited by

Ryan Bowd

With contributions from

Bo de Vries, Karen K. Lee,
Marylin Marx, and Paige Harvey

CRC Press
Taylor & Francis Group
Boca Raton London New York

CRC Press is an imprint of the
Taylor & Francis Group, an **informa** business

Designed cover image: Marco Mottura
Graphic Design and Illustration by: Verena Wurmser

First edition published 2024
by CRC Press
2385 Executive Center Drive, Suite 320, Boca Raton, FL 33431

and by CRC Press
4 Park Square, Milton Park, Abingdon, Oxon, OX14 4RN

CRC Press is an imprint of Taylor & Francis Group, LLC

Library of Congress Cataloging-in-Publication Data

Names: Wendt, Carolin, author.
Title: The pocket mentor for game community management / Carolin Wendt ;
edited by Ryan Bowd, with contributions from Bo de Vries, Karen K. Lee,
Marylin Marx, and Paige Harvey.
Other titles: Game community management
Description: First edition. | Boca Raton ; London : CRC Press, 2024. |
Series: The pocket mentors for games careers | Includes bibliographical
references and index.
Identifiers: LCCN 2023032025 (print) | LCCN 2023032026 (ebook) |
ISBN 9781032315973 (hbk) | ISBN 9781032315966 (pbk) | ISBN 9781003310488 (ebk)
Subjects: LCSH: Video games industry--Management.
Classification: LCC HD9993.E452 W356 2024 (print) | LCC HD9993.E452 (ebook) |
DDC 338.4/77948--dc23/eng/20231013
LC record available at https://lccn.loc.gov/2023032025
LC ebook record available at https://lccn.loc.gov/2023032026

ISBN: 978-1-032-31597-3 (hbk)
ISBN: 978-1-032-31596-6 (pbk)
ISBN: 978-1-003-31048-8 (ebk)

DOI: 10.1201/9781003310488

Typeset in Times
by KnowledgeWorks Global Ltd.

To everyone who lived their life being told something was out of reach and then boldly grasped it with both hands.

Contents

Acknowledgements

This book wouldn't have been possible without numerous people who played important roles in my life. It's not an easy feat to write a book while working full-time, and I wouldn't have embarked on this journey without the initial push and constant encouragement of my partner, Alessandro. Thank you for travelling the world with me, enduring my bad morning moods, and enabling my slightly unhinged book-buying habit.

I'll forever be grateful for Peter and Benjamin, who took a giant leap of faith and hired me as an intern after a Skype interview during my semester abroad. Without their support, I might have never entered the games industry or survived the first years.

Equal thanks go to Fabian and Christoph, who convinced me to apply to CD PROJEKT RED despite my imposter syndrome telling me I wouldn't stand a chance, and to Marcin and MPG for proving me wrong. All the past and present REDs who have made me learn more about myself and the industry. Bobby, I planned to spell your name in a cryptic message, but then I realised everyone should know how thankful I am for having my very own Yoda. Special thanks go to my #internationals, my Korean brothers, and my current and former RED sisters in spirit, who all inspire me for different reasons: Alicja, Amelia, Dominika, Hollie, Maha, Mariana, Mariko, Marta, Stephanie, and many more. Ryan – I owe you one drink and eternal gratitude for treating my words with your magic hands and turning this book into what it is today.

To my moderators and our community: I salute you for your incomparable passion and support.

Of course, I want to thank my whole family. Especially the infamous two: Mama, thank you for never questioning my love for games or my pivot away from politics. Sven, you know what you mean to me. Without you, I might have never found my love for games and continued to curate it by stealing yours and playing on your PC while you're in school.

My friends are the best people in the world: I cannot imagine life without you. I vow to be better at responding to messages. Thank you for existing, Akeel, Andi, Anna, Ann-Kathrin, Bente, Caro, Daniel, Eike, Federico, Feli, Fenja, Gnom, Jenny, Jonas, Jörg, Kirk, Lisa, Meli, Mona, Ron, Verena, and everyone who has enriched my life over the years. To Nahal and Pouya: we've met under the unluckiest circumstances, but you've shown me what true resilience looks like.

I'd be remiss not to thank CRC Press' Will and Simran, without whom *writing a book* would still be on my bucket list. To this day, I'm not quite sure how I deserved the honour to be approached by you, but I'll never forget it.

Last, I'm grateful to my peers, specifically my fellow CMs, who give me hope every day that our industry can improve. Bo, Karen, Marylin, and Paige: thank you for enriching this book with your invaluable perspectives and trusting me to handle them respectfully. This book wouldn't be the same without my many excellent peers who were generous with their time and wisdom and participated in my survey. Heartfelt thanks go out to Alexis Trust, Alina Ulrich, Andreas, Andrew, Anne van der Zanden, Benjamin, Chante Goodman, Christian Bergmann, Christopher Grünewald, Cole, Crew Dino, Darya, Fabien "Azureus" Vigneron, François, Fox, Liam Daniel Hart, Long Nguyen, Marion Mỹ Anh Baxerres, Mathes, Matzosaure, Nick Horodyvskyi, Rae Lyon, Rania, Robby Bisschop, Sasha JP, Suad Bensaud, Yegor Ostapenko, and the many more of you who preferred to remain anonymous.

To everyone who makes games: thank you for sharing your craft with the world and improving my life!

Selected Industry Acronyms

APAC	Asia-Pacific
B2B	Business-to-business
B2C	Business-to-consumer
CCU	Concurrent users
CEE	Central and Eastern Europe
CMS	Content management system
CPM	Cost-per-mille (cost per thousand) impressions
CPV	Cost per view
DAU	Daily active users
DLC	Downloadable content
DRM	Digital rights management
EMEA	Europe, the Middle East, and Africa
ESRB	Entertainment Software Ratings Board
KPI	Key performance indicators
LATAM	Latin America
MENA	Middle East and North Africa
NDA	Non-disclosure agreement
PEGI	Pan European Game Information
ROI	Return on investment
SEO	Search engine optimisation
SKU	Stock keeping unit

Guest Authors Biographies

Bo de Vries is Studio Communications Lead at Guerrilla in Amsterdam. With more than 10 years of experience working in Community Management, PR, and Influencer Marketing, she currently leads a small team of Community professionals on the Horizon franchise (Horizon Zero Dawn, Horizon Forbidden West, and Horizon Call of the Mountain), and is responsible for all internal and external communications about the company and its products.

Prior to her role at Guerrilla, Bo worked at Frontier (Planet Coaster, Planet Zoo, and Jurassic World Evolution) and Crytek (Crysis 3, Warface, and Ryse: Son of Rome).

Karen K. Lee is a seasoned game community developer in the gaming industry. She's worked at studios such as Gameloft, Ubisoft, and Respawn Entertainment, on titles such as Rainbow Six Siege, Assassin's Creed, and Apex Legends. She has also cofounded Project AWR, which works towards representation, awareness, and amplification of Asian women in and adjacent to gaming.

Marylin Marx is community management lead for Webedia Gaming in Munich. She oversees the community management for three of the largest German gaming websites: GameStar, GamePro, and MeinMMO. Previously, she was community editor for GameStar.de.

Paige Harvey is a disabled community manager who has worked in the games industry for over seven years. As a content creator, she's hosted panels and podcasts interviewing members of marginalised communities around the world while fundraising for related causes. Though she lives in the UK with her husband and two pet cats, you'll often find her travelling the worlds of Eorzea and Hyrule!

Meet the Author

1

1.1 WHY SHOULD YOU READ THIS BOOK?

Welcome! Thank you for picking up this book among all the things you could be doing with your life right now. I am excited that you're intrigued by the world of community management. Whether you are looking to break into the video games industry or are already working hard to create a great community, I hope I can be your companion for a part of your journey. Or maybe you merely wanted to see who had the audacity to write a guidebook for this field. The scope and details of the role change frequently – so what can you possibly learn from something as static as a book?

If I do my job correctly, you should have a better understanding of the aspects in Figure 1.1 after reading this book.

Still don't know why you should listen to me? Well, that's because you shouldn't!

1.2 DON'T LISTEN TO ME, PLEASE

I'm serious. Don't. Run away if someone tells you there's a simple trick to master any industry. If someone ever claims to know everything there is to know about community management, I'd urge you to at least raise a sceptical eyebrow.

In a way, my journey into the video games industry is typical and irregular at the same time. I never planned to be here. When I was in school, I never even thought about the possibility of earning money with games. But then, more than eight years ago, I abandoned the path in political science I'd

DOI: 10.1201/9781003310488-1

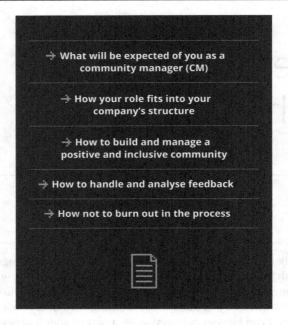

- → What will be expected of you as a community manager (CM)
- → How your role fits into your company's structure
- → How to build and manage a positive and inclusive community
- → How to handle and analyse feedback
- → How not to burn out in the process

FIGURE 1.1   Key things I hope you'll take away from this book.

laid out for myself; I thought, why not give myself a chance to really follow my dreams before committing to a "serious job"? Through luck, preparation, and passion, I managed to get an internship at a game culture foundation in Germany. From there I slowly carved out a career that has taken me from being a project manager to working in communication in an international AAA development studio. Today, I'm a lead in this company, responsible for a small, international team of community managers (CMs). I regularly work with partners from all areas of the industry, from community advocates and content creators to platform holders. And while I won't deny that I worked hard to be in this position, I developed a talent to be at the right location at the right moment, and I won't pretend that this applies to your situation.

At the same time, this kind of story is way more common than you might think. The unfair reality is that many industry members got lucky at the beginning, and this usually holds more truth the earlier someone joined the industry. The market is becoming increasingly competitive, and what worked 20, 10, or even 5 years ago will likely not be enough today.

No need to despair, though! I've gathered experiences and suggestions from many industry colleagues to point you in the right direction. These colleagues will also help to cover some areas that I frankly should not be writing about. The gaming industry is vast, and working in one of its corners does

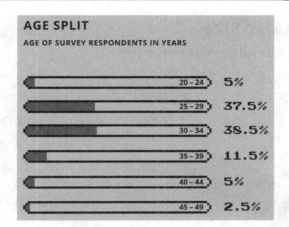

FIGURE 1.2   Survey participants show a wide split across age groups.

not automatically qualify me to speak about all of them. On top of including these peer articles, I've surveyed more than 40 industry professionals who worked as CMs in the past or still work in the role to supplement my perspective. As you can see in Figures 1.2 and 1.3, they are diverse both in age groups and genders represented.

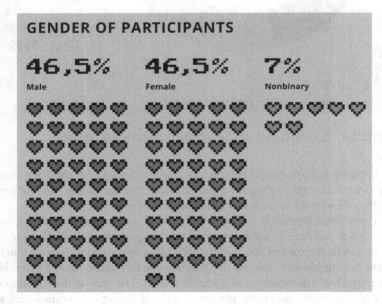

FIGURE 1.3   The CM role seems to see a more equal gender representation.

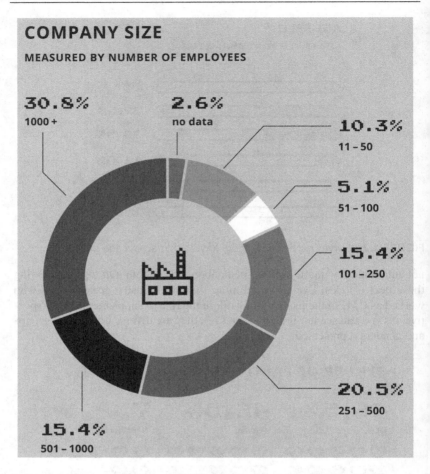

FIGURE 1.4   Surveyed CMs can be found in companies of all sizes.

Looking at professional parameters, Figures 1.4 and 1.5 show the company size of the studios the survey participants are employed at, and for how long they've worked in the industry at the time of the survey.

Throughout this book, you will find their expertise and advice for questions such as red flags in job listings, the most important skills for the role, or how to handle the mental strain of the job. The aim of this book is for you to receive the initial spark, the one that inspires you to venture out and assemble your individual community management toolkit. Use that as the foundation to build a network and create your own style of caring for communities so that you may tell others (including me) how to do it better in the future.

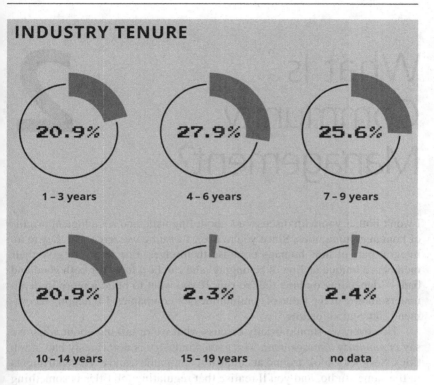

INDUSTRY TENURE

20.9% — 1 – 3 years

27.9% — 4 – 6 years

25.6% — 7 – 9 years

20.9% — 10 – 14 years

2.3% — 15 – 19 years

2.4% — no data

FIGURE 1.5 The survey includes people with a wide range of industry experience.

I'm writing this book because I would have loved to read it when I started working as a CM. While there are great books about the value of communities or the theory behind social media management, I couldn't find a book quite like this one; one that takes a good look at all my questions and then responds to them transparently and earnestly. Over the years, I've given talks to students and aspiring game developers, answering many private messages about getting a foot in the door. So many times, I found that these conversations repeated the same topics and talking points. Here, my goal is to have a conversation with all of you at once, in the hope that the knowledge gathered in this book can help as many of you as possible to find happiness and professional fulfilment in this exciting role. I would love to hear from you. And if you still think I'm being audacious by writing this book, honestly, so do I, but here we are. So, let's just embark on this journey together.

What Is Community Management?

2

I won't bother you with discussions about linguistic and sociological origins of human communities. Since you're here, I assume we agree that they're an integral part of how humans organise themselves, that they can give their members a unique feeling of belonging[1] and can be a force for both good and bad — depending on how they're run. If you want to build a more in-depth understanding of the value of communities for companies, I'll happily recommend some good reading.[2]

However, we should briefly discuss what we're talking about when we say *community management*. The games industry is notoriously bad at job titles. Seriously, look around at countries, companies, and even departments in the same studio, and you'll realise that regulating job titles is something the industry doesn't like doing. Two people could do the same job at two companies and have very different titles. Commonly, CMs are integrated into a company's communication department or into the broader marketing team. If you work for a smaller indie company or start-up, you might have all these roles wrapped into one (very stressed and caffeinated) person. Bigger publishers or development studios often have a dedicated community team. In this role, you'll craft methods of engaging different audiences, interact with them, and act as the connective tissue between them and the rest of the studio. You'll ensure their feedback is heard, understood by the development team, and, in turn, communicate company decisions to the community.

On top of that, you could be responsible for setting up and running streams, online and offline community events, social media strategies, and writing copy. Sometimes teams try to avoid hiring a dedicated CM and set up a Discord server or Twitter account where they post sparse updates. While the reasons behind a decision like this are usually financial, it's still a disservice to both the game they're making and the people who'll play it.

6

DOI: 10.1201/9781003310488-2

Some job listings will disagree with me but there are things a CM should not be asked to do. A CM isn't a magic billboard that attracts people to a game they've never heard about. If no one knows it yet, and the team wants to change that, they should hire a marketing manager. A CM is also not the clean-up crew. Even if they could do everything, the company should not expect CMs to be jack-of-all-trades that pick up all the work no one else wants to do. They're also not graphic designers. Can we create content for socials? Sure. Should we create all the marketing and social assets ourselves? No. Companies should hire professional graphic designers for that. Of course, there is nuance to this. In smaller companies, everyone usually fulfils more roles when needed. It's okay to work this way for a while, but please set boundaries for the long term.

2.1 COMMUNITY VERSUS SOCIAL MEDIA MANAGEMENT

Social media management is probably the role companies most often merge with community management, although they're technically two different roles with separate skill sets. Where social media management analyses the metrics of how posts perform, community management dives into the actual sentiment behind these numbers. As in my case and many more, though, the CM is also responsible for setting up social media channels, creating and executing a posting strategy, and interacting with players in comments and private messages. And if you're fortunate, you'll get to create and post a lot of memes.

To increase your chances of landing a job, I recommend not utterly despising social media. None of this means you'll have to be a public figure. There's room for all kinds of CMs; while some of the best ones I know have large followings, many interact only through their company accounts. Players know neither their real names nor their private social channels. Both versions are equally valid.

If your sole passion is planning social media campaigns, deep diving into the unique aspects of different platforms, and conceptualising Instagram Reels or TikTok videos, I'm unsure if the position is right for you. But I encourage you to read on and check for yourself. Even if you end up working as a social media manager in a company with dedicated CMs, those will be among your closest colleagues. Understanding each other's perspective will make everything easier.

2.2 AN ENTRY-LEVEL POSITION IN THE INDUSTRY?

Over the last few years, discussions have grown louder about properly recognising specific roles within game development. Unfortunately, there's often a barely hidden element of gatekeeping involved when some professions — like quality assurance (QA) or community management — are treated as a springboard for more "worthy" professions. It implies that the roles can be done by anyone and require no hard skills. While this is clearly not true, it would be false to say that community management isn't a great entry-level position. Being a CM is an excellent way to start working in the industry. Analogue to the famous phrase: it's relatively easy to learn its basics, but it's hard to master. To some degree, I understand those who want to work in games at all costs and take the job as a CM as an entryway. Getting a job in games is hard. However, I'll assume that something fascinates you about working with global communities, that you're burning to amplify the voices of players, and that you're considering turning this path into your career.

Because I promised you honesty: not everything is perfect. Often, the role *is* treated as a lesser contributor to a company's overall success. You'll probably be faced with decision-makers who don't understand the value of a great community and, by extension, your work. Your salary will likely be among the lowest in most studios. And clearly, there's still much work to be done across the industry to establish community management further as a valid career path of its own.

That all sounds a bit grim, doesn't it? You might be asking yourself why anyone, let alone you, should want to do this? I can answer that for you right here: because it's a fulfilling and challenging career. Interacting with passionate communities and feeling their excitement firsthand is really rewarding. As a CM, you'll be one of the most prominent voices of the company. Depending on the company, you'll be privy to confidential information that could shape the game's success. The company needs to trust your expertise on when to engage, when to flag issues, and when to disregard them. I don't know about you, but this sounds like quite an important role to me.

2.3 DO COMPANIES REALLY NEED THIS?

Yes. Today, more than ever. In an industry leaning increasingly towards community-centric gaming experiences and a society that highlights the importance of positive digital connection, I have no doubt that our job greatly benefits *every* for-profit gaming company. Community management is becoming more integral to overall marketing efforts. How to retain users and increase their loyalty, how to use word of mouth to its fullest extent, and how to improve the customer experience in a saturated and often impatient market are urgent questions for companies to answer.

On top of that, think of yourself as a crisis alert system. Of course, almost everyone working on a game will browse one or two social media platforms and grasp a partial sentiment overview. But relying on this is dangerously misleading. Comments on Reddit or Twitter threads alone never fully represent community sentiment. Acting upon these could cause panicked reactions, bad prioritisation, or wrong alignment with community needs. CMs are the closest of anyone in a company to their player base. They're gathering input from many sources, which allows them to understand what constitutes an actual crisis, and to develop a more holistic view of actual player priorities. Because they're so close to the community, they usually also gain a sixth sense of what could set them off, steer away from potentially problematic decisions, and prevent problems before they arise.

Now that you're hopefully even more secure that this career is worth pursuing, you may wonder how to get started. So let's dive into this together!

NOTES

---

1. You can find a great exploration of this in Bréné Brown's 2017 book, *Braving the Wilderness.*
2. For more senior advice on community management (not tailored to gaming), I'd recommend starting with the following: Jono Bacon: "People Powered," Carrie Melissa Jones: "Building Brand Communities. How Organizations Succeed by Creating Belonging." and David Spinks: "The Business of Belonging. How to Make Community Your Competitive Advantage."

To Study or Not to Study

3

A question I often get is: "Do I have to go to university?" Once I give my non-committal answer, people usually ask, "So, what do I need to do then?" It makes sense to want clear pathways to your goal, but things can get a bit murkier with community management. Or, to put it in a more positive light, there's no one right way to do it.

3.1 DO YOU NEED A UNIVERSITY DEGREE?

The very short answer is "no." If you want a more expansive response, I'd answer that sometimes you do, but it usually depends on your circumstances.

You probably won't find a course that teaches community management. Your local university may not even have a course focused on games. Do you feel exasperated yet? It's hard not to. But more universities are starting to offer degrees in digital marketing, social media, or digital communications. And if you truly want to immerse yourself in the topic and spend several years learning about the theoretical craft at the basis of the field, these degrees can create a great foundation. Before enrolling, though, please apply some due diligence, like so:

How long has the university, and this course specifically, existed? You might not think it matters, but once you're a student, you'll wish for proper reporting processes, a well-formed curriculum, and mechanisms to report potentially bad professors.

Does the university share the rough curriculum on its website? If yes, please at least skim the content to see if it feels relevant to your interests. If not, I would honestly suggest not to pursue it any further. A professional educational institution should make it possible for you in advance to find out – at least – the overall content outline of their courses.

Search for testimonials about the university and the course outside their controlled ecosystem. What do former or current students have to say? Are

DOI: 10.1201/9781003310488-3

the teachers qualified and people you'd like to learn from? Does the university have well-known industry partners offering workshops or internships? If the responses to all these questions satisfy you, you know what to do. But what if you're already in another university course or simply not interested in studying any of these courses? Don't worry; you can gain much transferable knowledge from most degrees – including self-organisation, writing, and data analysis. I'm always joking that my specialisation in diplomacy during my degree helps me deal with comments on social media. As long as you enjoy your studies, pursue it and focus on extracurricular activities that fit the required CM skillset.

Last, there is another pragmatic aspect. Depending on the type of company and the seniority level you aim to reach, companies will often ask for "a university degree in marketing, communications, or similar fields." For some companies, this is a hard criterion for entering the interview rounds. In others, it might just be nice to have. But all in all, having a degree is unlikely to hurt your chances.

At the same time, please don't feel forced to go to university to get a degree you don't need or want – especially if you're living in a country without free education. This requires a long-term commitment.

3.2 WHICH SKILLS DO YOU NEED?

This is probably the most-asked question. While a university degree is optional, numerous skills aren't. Unfortunately, there's a persistent stereotype that CMs require no "real" skills. Sometimes people assume that the job *only* demands soft skills, which stems from the outdated belief that soft skills are less valuable than hard skills. In reality, being a CM requires a healthy mix of both.

Since the role and requirements vary depending on the company, I scouted industry job aggregators, career pages of numerous companies, and platforms such as LinkedIn to gather CM job listings to present you with the most thorough picture. I analysed listings from 62 gaming companies across five continents, from some of the biggest AAA publishers to small indie developers. No company was taken into consideration more than once. After crossing out all criteria that would allow identification, I condensed them into 34 *mandatory* soft and hard skills and 16 *desirable* skills. You'll notice some overlaps that stem from how important different companies found specific skillsets. Let's dive in.

The following skills presented in Table 3.1 were listed by gaming companies in late 2022 for CM roles. They're listed in descending order of mentions (with the percentage in relation to the total number of job listings):

TABLE 3.1   Mandatory and desirable skills in recent job listings for CMs

SKILL	IN %	IMPORTANCE
Excellent written & verbal communication	79	Mandatory
Copywriting for different audiences & formats	79	
Social platforms: theoretical knowledge	64.5	
Excellent English proficiency (written & verbal)	58.1	
Social platforms: practical experience[1]	56.5	
Structured & analytical work style	51.6	
Independent worker	51.6	
Strong passion for video games[2]	48.4	
Experience managing large online communities	38.7	
Games industry & business knowledge[3]	35.5	
Strong understanding of key performance indicators & social analytics tools	33.9	
Ability to create & present data-based reports	33.9	
Team player (incl. cross team)	33.9	
Flexible mindset & able to work in a *fast-paced environment*	25.8	
Proactivity	24.2	
Streaming experience/able to represent the company on camera	24.2	
Excellent proficiency in a second language besides English	22.6	
Experience building professional community campaigns	22.6	
Excellent knowledge of MS Office tools or equivalents	22.6	
Knowledge of Photoshop & Adobe Creative Suite	21	
Experience communicating via brand channels	19.4	
Experience in partnership & content creator management	19.4	
Creativity	17.7	
Ability to travel internationally to represent the company[4]	11.3	
Empathy/high emotional intelligence	11.3	
Project management skills	11.3	
Technical skills with stream setups & OBS proficiency	9.7	
Knowledge of content management systems & basic HTML	8.1	

(Continued)

TABLE 3.1   *(Continued)*

SKILL	IN %	IMPORTANCE
Team leadership & mentoring experience	8.1	
Ability to work long hours and weekends[5]	6.5	
Experience in event planning & execution	6.5	
Open-mindedness	3.2	
Experience working with development teams	1.6	
Minimum intermediate proficiency in a third language	1.6	
Graphic design skills	33.9	Desirable
Experience in short- and long-form video creation	33.9	
Experience setting up & hosting live streams	25.9	
Game industry knowledge	16.1	
Intermediate skills in a second language other than English	11.3	
Experience working with content creators	9.7	
Able to work in a fast-paced environment	8.1	
Project management experience	8.1	
Proficiency with JIRA, Confluence, & Sharepoint	6.5	
Experience with social listening & reporting tools	6.5	
Team management & leadership experience[6]	6.5	
Knowledge of a third language	6.5	
Experience running online gaming communities	4.8	
Ability to sit still[7]	1.6	
Creativity	1.6	
Paid media experience	1.6	

Don't fret if you're missing some of these skills. I doubt anyone looking to break into the industry fulfils all these requirements. The people hiring for these positions probably don't either. To a certain degree, it has become a meme that job listings are unrealistic; you don't have to fulfil everything the company asks for. A good rule of thumb is that you should feel (somewhat) comfortable with six or seven out of ten requirements and aim to acquire the remaining ones on the job, if necessary. If you bring some of the desirables, it can also outweigh a lack of some core requirements.

To cross-check these results from job listings with lived experience, I've asked my peers what they believe are the most essential skills for CMs and compiled them in Figure 3.1.

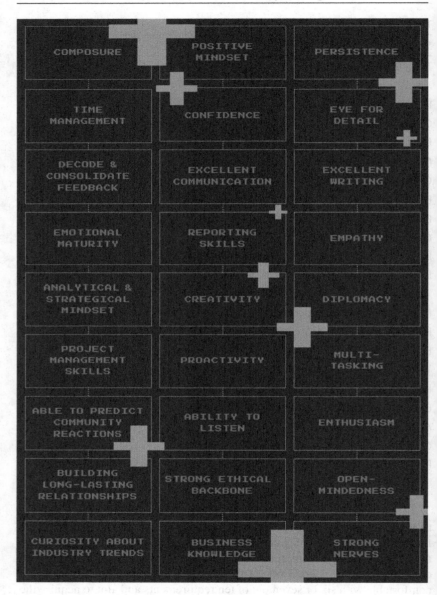

FIGURE 3.1 Most valuable CM skills according to the experience of my survey participants.

Let's dive deeper and talk about how you can work on some of the most high-demand skills.

Language and communication skills are crucial for any CM. If you're not a native English speaker, prioritise polishing your proficiency level. You must be comfortable speaking and writing both in professional and colloquial English at a very high level. In addition, the 58.1% requirement is a bit misleading; most jobs don't even list it as a requirement, instead assuming it as a given because of the company location. With the industry being as international as it is and companies recruiting talent from all over the world, English will be the company language in most cases, even if the studio is based in a non-English-speaking country. Whether you're a native speaker or not, you should start working on copywriting samples if you haven't written for another job before. Imagine that you have to write social media copy or newsletters for your favourite games. How would you write posts for a sale, a release announcement, or a community activation? Include different platforms since the tone and limitations vary significantly between places such as Twitter or Pinterest. If you want to go the extra mile, you could create a personal website where you write articles, commentary, or creative pieces. Of course, you might not write newsletters or pen Steam descriptions, but it doesn't hurt to grasp or hone these skills. If you're like me and English isn't your native language, you should multiply this requirement by two. Many companies seek regional representatives to cover community management in certain regions like DACH, LATAM, CEE, MENA, and many more.[8] If you possess native language skills in any of the main languages the games industry works in, this can vastly increase your chances of landing a job. On the other hand, it requires that you have an excellent written and verbal command of that language too – and can translate to and from English. On rare occasions, this might even apply to a third language, but that isn't something I'd recommend putting your energy into. If you happen to be trilingual, awesome! If not, don't sweat it.

Communication encompasses various other skills that are less tangible than language proficiency – but just as important. It may sound easy, but you'll need to identify the needs of thousands of people with different backgrounds and talk about your company's plans in a way that's understandable to all of them. At the same time, you need to know how to create tailored messaging for subgroups. If you're handling a company's Discord server or responding to private messages on social media, this comes with the added pressure that people might take screenshots of your words and circulate them. As a result, you should work on a clear and precise writing style while maintaining a unique tone. One of the most significant abilities you can develop is creating a recognisable and exciting tone for your channels without alienating parts of your audience or creating issues for the company. How? That's the million-dollar question, and you most likely won't master it at the beginning of your career (if you do, please teach me). Follow channels of games and companies you like or have heard good things about. Note which accounts make you pause, engage, or giggle to yourself. Whatever sparks joy, so to speak. Once you've gathered some examples, identify what makes them unique, how they talk about their games, and, most importantly, how they address their communities. From inside jokes and specific lingo to a full-fledged persona, you can learn much from observing your (future) peers. Get into the habit of writing in different voices. If you already have companies in mind that you want to apply to, write some copy for their games. When I applied to my current company, I included example postings across different channels that showed what to expect if they hired me. Rather than telling hiring managers that you can do it, demonstrate it!

That leads us to the second biggest set of skill requirements – tool and platform knowledge. As I mentioned, a lot of companies will expect you to also handle social media management (or don't understand the difference), so you should acquire a thorough knowledge of different social media platforms. How do audiences differ between Facebook and Instagram? What's the accepted tone on Twitter versus TikTok? You don't have to understand their fabled algorithms, but you should understand how the leading platforms work and pay attention to what content performs well and why. If you want to build this skill, create accounts on two or three platforms and fill them with content. By no means does this mean you have to amass significant follower counts. Instead, you should get a feel for content strategy – how to get into consistent posting, how to write, and communicate. What you post about is entirely up to you. Do you work for your university's newspaper? Take on its channels. Are you an avid lover of taking gaming screenshots? Share them online. Do you love bread and taking pictures of it? I salute you. Once you start this process, familiarise yourself with the platforms' built-in analytics tools to check off another required skill. Delve into the different menus to understand the difference between reach, engagement, and click rates. Go through demographic data and see how those numbers come to be – and what influences them. Wrap your head around the data. This will build the foundation for reporting key performance indicators (KPIs) to stakeholders in the company. I don't think you need to join with a proven track record of reporting on the data. You can learn and demonstrate this on the job since every company has a different approach, templates, and tools anyway. Getting acquainted with the terminology and the logic behind it should be enough.

Please just keep one thing in mind: keep those social media accounts presentable and professional in tone. You can post memes, of course – that's normal in numerous communities – but remember that communication professionals will scroll through them to evaluate whether you're suited to take over their brand channels. The same applies to your private accounts. Even if you don't list them on your resume, hiring managers will most likely do their due diligence and find them. In one of many examples I've heard over the years, an otherwise promising hiring process was abandoned when it turned out that the candidate had previously sent a public death threat on a social media platform. I know this can seem intrusive – but remember that how you conduct yourself online will reflect on the company once they hire you. More than once, individuals' social channels have created issues for companies. You should still be yourself, as long as you're a decent person.

Speaking of decent: there are some characteristics and soft skills companies often want to see in their CMs. If you want to be a lone wolf, completely independent from other departments, this role won't satisfy your desires. Game development is a collaborative endeavour. Working well in diverse teams is thus an explicit requirement of more than a third of all listings. If you haven't worked with other people during your education or as part of hobbies, join activities you're passionate about that will allow you to train that muscle. It's essential to understand what motivates other people, how to work with those who have different perspectives, and when to compromise. It'll be better to learn this in a lower-stakes environment rather than being thrown into complex issues at work.

In my experience, a family of skills that's becoming increasingly more important is everything connected to live streaming and videos. Social media platforms and games marketing have shifted towards video assets. Companies are looking for that rare person to set up their Twitch channel, plan and host their streams, and edit the final videos for the YouTube account – which they'd like that same person to manage, too. Of course, CMs shouldn't have to do all these things, and bigger companies will have video editors, tech experts, and spokespeople for on-screen appearances. However, having a solid foundation in this area might be the deciding factor for hiring you over someone else. One quarter of all job listings already explicitly lists it as an obligatory requirement. There are a couple of options for you to work on this skill; if you decide, you may want to be a public-facing CM. If you're intrigued by the possibility of being in the public eye, work on getting comfortable in front of a camera. That should be the first step.

If you use video-based social media channels privately, create videos. Don't worry about fancy equipment or high production values. Initially, it's all about learning the basics. Have a go at creating Instagram stories where you talk into the camera. Edit short videos and post them. If this feels like too much too fast, start with the absolute basics and train! Record yourself talking in front of your phone. Look into the lens and improvise. Next time, maybe write a short script, tell a joke – whatever you do, just get used to the feeling of speaking to a camera. The actual final boss is, of course, creating your own Twitch or YouTube channel. I'm not the right person to coach you on this, but plenty of free online resources can get you started. Creating these accounts is free, and I'd only spend money once you realise that it's something you're enjoying and can see yourself doing for a longer time. Remember: this should be fun. Obtaining technical skills such as setting up the channel, writing descriptions and choosing appropriate categories, using video editing and streaming software, working with thumbnails, and how analytics work on video platforms will be an added benefit.

That last sentence leads us to a general area of expertise you can develop without a job in the industry – proficiency with specific tools and software. I've already mentioned OBS (short for Open Broadcaster Software), which is extremely useful if you want to get into video streaming. Apart from that, the requirements from the job listings above reveal three main skill areas: MS Office tools or similar (22.6%), Adobe Photoshop, or other graphic editing software (21%), and slightly less sought-after at 8.1% is basic HTML knowledge and being able to work in a Content Management Systems (CMS). For all three of these areas, there are free ways to train your metaphorical muscles. Being a graphic designer is a separate skillset from being a CM, yet many companies prefer if you could create social media assets yourself. Whether your future company requires you to edit images or not, basic graphic design skills will probably be helpful. If you want to use a similar tool to Adobe Photoshop but don't have money to spend, I'd recommend GIMP. While the features aren't the same – and the user interface looks different – the skills you obtain will be transferable.

A perfect way to apply this skill is by working on your own website and creating assets for it. It helps sharpen your design skills while also allowing you to gather experience with basic HTML and CMS. You can either create a portfolio or just make a website for any topic that interests you. There are both cheap or free services to create a website, and you can use them to familiarise yourself with how to set up content on the backend of a website, plan and write articles, and use images to illustrate your arguments.

If you're not already doing it, start reading about the industry. Not only does it help you with your future job, but it's also a commonly cited requirement for CMs (35.5%). Become knowledgeable about the most successful games of the last year, upcoming releases in the next quarters, and overall genre trends. Rather than learning only about games, investigate industry trends, learn about different business models, and try to wrap your head around technology and hardware trends. Why is this relevant? Because you have to ensure that your work follows company strategies in a broader industry context, and it's crucial that you're not only talking from a fan's perspective. One company put it very well in their listing: you have to *be able to balance community needs against the business' goals.* Various media outlets and content creators present excellent information on these areas[9]. If you want to work as a games professional, elevating your knowledge about the industry beyond being a consumer is something you should start doing as soon as you can.

As you can see, you don't have to wait for someone to give you a chance and hire you, you can start developing many of the required skills immediately. This way, once that dream job appears on your radar, you'll hopefully feel much more qualified. My fingers are crossed for you.

3.3 ALTERNATIVE ENTRY WAYS

Earlier, I told you that a university degree won't be your only way to become a CM. But if not through the academic path, how is it possible? I don't know about your country of birth, but in mine, the school system didn't offer an honest look at all the opportunities ahead of us. The choice seemed daunting. No matter how you looked at it, you had to do either an apprenticeship in a more specialised role or attend university. Of course, I sincerely hope things have been modernised since then. But to a certain extent, schools will never be able to properly depict an ever-evolving career landscape in our digital age. Why am I going on this tangent? Mainly, I want to comfort you. It isn't your fault if you feel lost or didn't consider following the gaming path.

There are alternative ways to bolster your CV and get noticed. Let me give you some examples. All of these stem from cases I've witnessed myself more than once over the last couple of years.

3.3.1 Become a Moderator for a Gaming Company

I don't know how I'd survive without my moderators. This might sound like an exaggeration, but I can assure you that, at times, this has felt true. For any game of a certain size, a few moderators usually help keep their spaces safe and welcoming. Of course, certain platforms have built-in moderation tools available, but they're no competition for the nuances and subtlety of a skilled person. And that's where you come in! You can reach out to companies politely, mention that you really like their games (please don't lie about this) and that you'd be more than happy to help them as moderator.

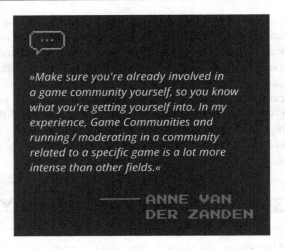

»Make sure you're already involved in a game community yourself, so you know what you're getting yourself into. In my experience, Game Communities and running / moderating in a community related to a specific game is a lot more intense than other fields.«

———— ANNE VAN DER ZANDEN

Once you're moderating for a company, you'll gather valuable experience. You'll get to know the community from a very intimate perspective, enhance your communication skills, train your stress resistance, and think on your feet. In addition, you'll be close to the CMs – so if there's ever a vacancy opening at their company, chances are high they'll think of you. And if they don't, the experiences are still yours.

3.3.2 Be an Active Community Member (for the Company of Your Dreams)

I'll let you in on a secret. I'll open a community wiki if I want to quickly check something about our games. I know for a fact that a lot of game devs do the same. The passion and attention to detail inherent in gaming communities are incredible, and they don't go unnoticed by studios and their employees. If there's a game you really enjoy, engage with it. Contribute actively to the community. Build or maintain community wikis, create cosplays, become a virtual photographer, or be a very helpful person on social channels or forums responding to other people's questions.

Try whatever brings you joy and taps into a skillset you want to build. I'm not saying it's your direct ticket to employment. However, I know numerous people who have been hired based on such actions – from cosplayers and virtual photographers to modders and streamers of the game. Their work in the community helped them be discovered, and their skills secured the job.

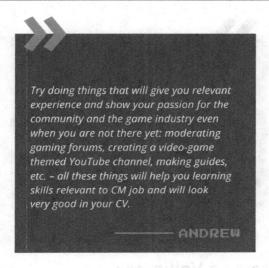

Try doing things that will give you relevant experience and show your passion for the community and the game industry even when you are not there yet: moderating gaming forums, creating a video-game themed YouTube channel, making guides, etc. – all these things will help you learning skills relevant to CM job and will look very good in your CV.

ANDREW

Even if the company whose community you're engaging with doesn't reach out to you after a while, you'll still develop essential skills that can help you find something else.

3.3.3 Gather Adjacent Experience

Even if you know in the deepest, darkest corner of your heart that you want to be a CM, you might not find a position immediately. It's absolutely okay to wait, continue searching, and try getting interviews for your dream role. If you can't afford or don't want to, you can also accept other jobs and work towards obtaining relevant experience within that position. See if you can take on projects that will help you build up your skills. By doing so, you can see which tasks you enjoy – and even while you're not employed as a CM, you can still gain relevant experience. Keep track of all the different things you do and bring them up during a performance review. If your employer sees your work and engagement, you might be able to discuss a role change within the same company. If that's impossible or you want to leave, start looking for a CM opportunity, now equipped with more professional experience.

Similarly, many people enter the games industry via internships during their education or after graduation. Keep your eyes open for company pro- grammes; very often, they're willing to bring you on as a regular employee if you prove yourself.

Get into the industry by doing some volunteering for small structures like small esport teams or journalist websites.

——— FABIEN
»AZUREUS«
VIGNERON

3.3.4 Become a Volunteer

If you can spare some time without getting paid, one way of improving your skills and making new contacts is to volunteer. Beware: volunteering doesn't mean doing jobs for free that companies could afford paying for. Don't sell yourself below value – and don't ruin the market for others. Instead, look for game industry events or initiatives with cool mission statements but not in the financial position to afford full-time CMs. They can be pretty hard to find, which is one of the reasons why they might need your help as a communicator.

Contact them to see if they want someone to help. Don't be shy to mention that you hope to work in the industry full-time and want to gather experience. Explain what tasks you could take on. The options are manifold. You could handle their social media channels, manage their website, work with creators to spread the message, create live streams, assist with event management, and more. If they onboard you as a volunteer, beyond valuable experience, this could provide an excellent catalyst for building your network.

.NOTES

1. The most listed channels in 2022 are Instagram, TikTok, and Discord.
2. Some listings require certain genres/platforms, but I summarised them into one point.

3. Notably different phrasing than the "passion requirement." Listings went into detail about understanding the industry and "market trends."
4. Not included is the requirement to travel to company headquarters.
5. Ouch. Some of these companies listed "great work-life balance" as a benefit, too.
6. The only time I felt tempted to name a company was when I found a job listing for a junior CM asking for leadership experience.
7. My favourite requirement.
8. The games industry adores (!) acronyms and I've provided an overview of some of the more common ones at the start of this book. These describe some of the ways in which we have sliced up the globe: DACH (Germany, Austria, Switzerland), LATAM (Latin America), CEE (Central Eastern Europe), and MENA (Middle East and North Africa).
9. While it's hard to pick just one, I personally learn(ed) a tremendous amount from the good people at GamesIndustry.biz.

Hunting for the Perfect Job

4

4.1 WHERE TO FIND JOBS

Okay, you've decided that this is the career you want to pursue. You think you have the skills that companies need – or you're motivated to develop them – but how do you find a job? At this point, I'll repeat something, and I'm sorry for bringing the mood down: getting an entry-level job in the gaming industry is difficult. This was true in 2015 when I started, and the demand has only increased since. Even big studios usually only have a handful of community roles available – most of which are, on average, senior positions. Why am I telling you this? Because I don't want you to lose hope! I want you to be armed with as much knowledge as possible. The jobs are out there, but you'll have to endure not getting any responses, or only getting negative ones, for a while. Please don't let it discourage you. With time, you'll manage to find one of those coveted positions.

Pursue it from a couple of angles. Min-max[1] your chances! If you don't have a job yet but have a small network, let people know you're looking for one. It sounds too simple, doesn't it? But people in the industry often reach out to others to ask them for recommendations. It has happened to me several times. If others ask me if I know someone looking for a job, I need to know you're one of them. Otherwise, I don't know how to pitch you for that position. Of course, how you weave it into conversations depends on the context – but dropping an "if you hear about someone looking for a CM" is generally accepted when talking to others. As much as it seems unfair to newcomers, connections are the best way to hear about new opportunities, and you shouldn't feel bad for making use of yours.

If you don't know anyone yet, you're not out of luck. While it's unlikely that headhunters will proactively search for juniors, it's helpful to start building your online representation. Preferences vary, but I recommend creating a LinkedIn

DOI: 10.1201/9781003310488-4

account and filling it out in accordance with your resumé. Treat it as a professional base for your job hunt that enables you to reach out to recruiters. Similarly, across social networks from Facebook to Discord, the industry has created groups to discuss and share opportunities, with many open for people who want to start out. Whenever you can, join these groups and introduce yourself.

My third recommendation is probably the most straightforward: keep an eye on career portals. Write down companies you'd love to work for, have won awards for being good employers, or are active in your local community. Spend some time visiting their websites and bookmarking their career sites to receive updates straight from the source. Make it as easy as possible for yourself to check options at companies you're interested in. Once you see an opening, apply. To quote a hallmark moment of our culture: just do it! On top of company websites and LinkedIn, there are aggregate websites that companies use to advertise their listings; make sure to check those as well and set alerts for your keywords. Remember that there are usually dedicated websites for different countries, so make sure to search for the ones that apply to you.[2] I'll once again plug GamesIndustry.biz because they not only have a dedicated section where you can look for industry jobs and filter by remote work possibilities or locations, but they also have great general resources about the industry and allow you to get in touch with potential employers.

4.2 HOW TO DECIPHER JOB POSTINGS

Job listings. The bane of many an existence. They are frequently ridiculous, and there's no defending them ("five years of experience, a degree, and two games shipped for a junior position"), but there's usually a logic to them. Once you learn how to read them, you can use them to your advantage when crafting your application.

Look up a listing for any job you find interesting. If you're anything like me when I started, you might feel inadequate, but I'll reiterate one truth that changed my approach: companies ask for more than they need. It's as simple as that. A long time ago, a senior in the industry told me to think about job listings like hidden public relations (PR). Some companies are notorious for their requirements and tricky technical tests. Surely, they only take the best, which obviously reflects in their high-quality products. That sentiment is by design. People in hiring positions draw an image of their ideal candidate and add some nice-to-have sprinkles. They're fully prepared to interview candidates who don't fulfil all requirements. So, apply even if you don't. Seriously. Write down the requirements. Check off all the ones you know how to do or those you don't but have done something similar. It bears repeating: do you tick off six or seven items out of ten? Then you're perfectly qualified and I urge you to apply. Furthermore, you can learn numerous skills outside the specific job scope and use your life or previous work experience. Just think about how you present this when applying. Carefully read not only the formal list of requirements, but also any section such as *what we are looking for* or *your responsibilities*. Include aspects from those in your application. For example, one company said something like: *we want you to be excited about the process of figuring things out together with us.* Sounds nice, right? Well, it can be, but it also means this is a place without formal processes and a big guarantee that things will often happen in a last-minute scramble. So, you have to embrace the chaos and thrive in it! Even better, maybe you have experience with settings that lacked pipelines for teamwork, and you have successfully implemented them. For example, did you improve how your school newspaper worked and managed to keep deadlines? Add it as a cheeky story in your cover letter or interview. Do you have an example where everything imaginable went wrong, yet you still managed to hand in a project? Talk about it! A personal warning, though: the kind of company asking for this can be a stressful place to work for junior people who need more guidance because, usually, places like this don't have the best onboarding material or processes either.

Companies often ask for a *proactive approach*. Simply said, they don't want you to wait for someone to tell you what to do or which problem to solve; they want you to develop additional projects yourself. If you see this in a job listing, include an example in which you did precisely that. Perhaps the database for contacts at your previous internship lacked efficiency, and you improved it without being asked. Or maybe you did some research on a topic that later helped your previous employer or group. These are great examples of proactivity.

Several companies mention that you need to *address and solve difficult situations within the community*. Again, think of examples from your education or training where you mediated arguments. Or maybe you're a member of an MMO guild or Minecraft server and settled a dispute over resource distribution. Bringing those experiences up in a professional interview might sound weird, but they're still valid. Prioritise professional ones wherever possible, but don't shy away from personal ones – this shows the interviewer that you can solve problems creatively and come up with quick solutions in stressful moments. It'll always be better than being asked about it, stammering that you haven't faced this situation yet or not even talking about it in the interview and being rejected due to a lack of relevant experience. Read the job listing carefully and brainstorm about yourself. I'm sure you have more expertise than you give yourself credit for.

Now that you hopefully understand job listings better, let me say one last thing. Please watch out for yourself and set boundaries. I'm not trying to throw any shade at companies that do this, but job titles such as "Community Brand Marketing Manager" evoke mostly one thing in my mind: burnout. If you feel that the role asks for three or more different positions, that's usually because it is. As hard as you might try, you won't be able to dedicate yourself fully to any of these positions –or if you could, probably only to the great detriment of your mental or physical health. If you want your first foray into community management to be a positive experience, avoid roles with issues like this baked in. If the job listing is vague and you don't quite understand what the company is looking for – they probably don't know, and you should be aware of that. In these situations, there's either no one in the company that understands the position – or there is, but they want too many things at once and cannot fully decide what they'd like you to do. In both cases, ask detailed questions during the interview. If you're wondering about other possible red flags, here are some of the things other CMs have told me:

- Being asked to be a community and social media manager at once, plus a customer support specialist, influencer manager, translator, copywriter, graphic designer, video producer, and PR expert.
- Junior roles requiring years of experience or the execution of high-level strategy.
- Always-on requirement.
- "We are a family here."
- Certain keywords like *rockstar* or *Swiss Army knife*.
- Payment offered in cryptocurrency.
- Metrics and data analytics as first on the list of responsibilities instead of focusing mainly on sentiment.
- Any mentions of long work hours, expected overtime, or disparaging statements about work-life balance.
- Unspecific or very general job listings. It usually shows no one understands what you're supposed to do.
- No benefits, including only minimum vacation days.
- The same or similar positions posted multiple times by the same company.
- Requiring software skills not applicable to the job.

I understand how urgent it can feel to find your first job. We need money to survive, after all. However, please know your worth. Sadly, so many people have bad experiences with the industry, but avoiding such red flags can help you have great ones instead.

To end this section, I quote Alexis Trust, comms manager at Chucklefish. When I asked what she would like to get off her chest, she responded:

> When applying for roles, reach out to current AND former staff to get an idea of how the company treats its employees. Whilst roles are rare, the damage 1 year in a terrible role to get your foot in the door isn't worth your well-being. Not only will you learn bad habits, but you'll take that trauma to your next role and will have to spend time unlearning that bad juju. It can lead to self-sabotage.

4.3 HOW MUCH MONEY SHOULD I ASK FOR?

I can feel you're slowly getting tired of this answer, but how much money you should ask for depends on many factors. For instance, I don't know which country you're living in or where the company offices are, and this is one of the biggest influences on your potential salary.

There's one thing I want to reiterate for full transparency. On average, CM roles are at the lower end of the salary spectrum in the games industry. It's still possible to find CM jobs that pay very well, and with more recognition of the field, salaries might increase in the future, but approach this with realistic expectations. I understand that categories such as low and high are incredibly subjective and hard to grasp without concrete numbers. But keep in mind that these are constantly changing. It's more critical for you, in the long run, to understand how to get what's right for you rather than fixating on any numbers I could provide you with that would be outdated within a year. Once you break into the industry, you'll realise people love sharing information with each other. Because salaries are largely shrouded in secrecy, industry professionals have created numerous spreadsheets and websites for different roles and regions where people can anonymously submit their salaries.[3]

An exciting development of the last couple of years is that some countries and states now require companies to include a salary range in their listings. Personally, I hope that this practice will become more normalised, as it evens out the playing field and helps contribute to pay equality. Still, some ranges are incredibly wide. Which end of the spectrum you fall on depends on a few factors, such as years of experience, your level of education, and negotiation skills. This leads me to an important point when talking about salaries. Don't be shy when talking about money. If you're unsatisfied with the amount offered, there's always room to discuss it. I was afraid of this in the past, thinking my question might ruin an otherwise great interview and close the door for me. Please let me free you from that fear. If a company wants to hire you and sends you the offer, simply trying to renegotiate your salary politely won't make them reconsider the overall offer. Maybe they'll tell you there's no wiggle room in the budget. Perhaps they'll try to meet you somewhere in the middle – that's a success! If you want to renegotiate your salary, research and know what you can ask for. Is your preferred salary twice as high as the offered one? Ouch. Please check whether your expectations may be set a bit too high or if the company is trying to severely underpay you. I use two main criteria for my (realistic) *target* salary: what's the average pay for this role? What's the cost of life in the city I'd be living in?

Regarding the average pay, you can also check websites such as Glassdoor, where current and former employees can anonymously submit their salaries. You can search for specific companies to check their salaries or search for the position in your city to get examples more tailored to you. LinkedIn also allows you to search for salaries. I've found numbers on Glassdoor to be more in line with other information I had, but I'd recommend checking as many options as possible. Just keep in mind that you should always examine the available information for biases and subjectivity. The most likely people to leave a review are people at the lowest and highest ends of the satisfaction spectrum. Just think about restaurant reviews on Google Maps; you hate or love it, or you usually don't care enough to post about it. This heavily impacts what you can gleam from portals like these, so if you have the opportunity and you've already started building your own network – ask people. I know not everyone feels comfortable talking about their income (and some companies also try to prevent pay transparency). Still, if you tell people you're trying to find a realistic starting salary, I'd estimate that more people will be willing to share.

Please remember that salary doesn't always equal salary. Numerous things impact how much of that gross income will end up in your pockets as actual discretional income. For example, what may put you into the bracket of the top 5% incomes in one region of the world might not even finance a one-bedroom apartment in a different country. In some countries, you'll have to factor in steep taxation rates, while others rely on you to put money aside for health insurance or pension funds, and an emergency will cost you dearly. Does the company cover healthcare? Commuting cost? Education costs? All these questions impact what makes a *great* salary, so check the company website for additional perks and benefits and ask about them during the interview process. Companies love advertising them, so finding them shouldn't be hard.

In the end, considering a move to another city – let alone country – can seem daunting. How are you supposed to know how expensive things really are? The good thing is that you're not the only person in this situation. There are a lot of expats working all around the world who share their experiences online. My personal favourite resource (used mainly for daydreaming) is Numbeo.[4] It's a community-driven website that offers living expense calculations and allows you to directly compare two cities for different criteria. It covers everything from the average cost of a city-centre apartment to the price of restaurants and the cost of bread. Because it relies on individual submissions, it comes with the drawback that popular destinations have more entries, and thus a more reliable average, than cities where people seldom move. Still, it's a special tool for understanding how much you'll really need.

As with the data on Glassdoor and other portals, keep in mind that those numbers will always contain some bias, so only use them as an estimate. Gather all this information and calculate your personal thresholds. What is your dream salary? Write it down and keep it as an aspiration. What's the minimum required salary you can afford to live on? Write it down. Add enough money to account for savings, unforeseen spendings, and emergencies (don't work for the bare minimum!), and politely refuse anything below that number. Finally, write down a comfortable salary for you to live on that allows you to save some money, repay loans, and generally enjoy life. Work with this salary range as the baseline for your negotiations.

To close this chapter, I want to get one thing off my chest: I hope that this chapter will be irrelevant someday soon. Salaries, especially those you earn when entering a company, determine so much of your path. I don't believe it should be up to individuals to demystify payments. Instead, I'd like the industry to move towards fair and transparent compensation and to proactively share salary ranges. I know – I'm an optimist. Until that magical day arrives, I hope these tips will help you. Go get that money!

4.4 NETWORKING – IT'S NOT THAT BAD

Let me tell you a secret. Two, actually. Firstly, most people have a deep hatred for networking. Secondly, most people completely misunderstand it. It isn't about collecting business cards at parties with mediocre finger food, at least not if you want to do it properly. Networking has a bad reputation. It reeks of opportunism and sucking up to people. In reality, it's about making genuine connections based on shared interests, respect, or simply sympathy. We just call it networking because those connections live within the professional sphere of one's life. If you want to get your first job in the industry, you must build relationships with others in the field. Not only can they help you in your quest to find one of these coveted jobs, but you can also help each other by providing feedback, reviewing your applications, or even launching projects together that can provide valuable experience. When put like this, networking doesn't sound so horrible anymore, does it? As a wise man once said: it's dangerous to go alone.

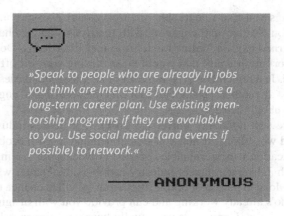

Now you may wonder how this networking thing works in practice. If you can attend in-person events, going to conventions and industry conferences is probably the best way to introduce yourself to other professionals. Attend talks and panel discussions, use the opportunity to ask questions, and approach speakers afterwards about their topics. In some cities, dedicated job fairs might also target (soon-to-be) graduates, offering portfolio and resumé reviews and allowing you to connect with talent acquisition teams. If you don't know where you can find events in your area, start by searching for "[city name+] Dev Meetup" or a local IGDA chapter.[5] Once you find an event you'd like to attend, remember that other attendees will also likely be nervous – or at least remember how nervous they felt their first time. It's improbable that people will not try to integrate you if you approach them. And if you're still hesitant, then the best option to feel comfortable at these events is to bring a friend!

Should personal circumstances or a lack of accessibility provisions at the venue prohibit you from attending these events – or the idea of being around this many people exhaust you – please don't be disheartened. An increasing number of events are slowly introducing digital elements, including dedicated networking sessions. Use these digital opportunities as much as you can! The benefit is that you're no longer limited to events within your range of transportation; in fact, now you can also sign up for global ones. There are also several Discord servers for CMs you can find with a simple Google search to connect with your peers, ask for advice, and organise digital exchanges. You can also start by engaging with other people's content online. Share some genuine feedback or appreciation via comments or DMs. Networking can be as simple as this. Don't expect anything in return; do it to connect with people who do things you find remarkable or inspirational. I've met many incredible people on Twitter, and engaging with their posts and exchanging DMs over time turned us from online randoms to real-life friends. Don't discount digital networking because that would mean closing yourself off from many great people. Just remember to be mindful of people's boundaries; someone's personal post about their pets or children isn't the best time to engage them in a discussion about their job.

If you're still attending university, check if it invites industry experts for talks and workshops. If not, you should demand it – it'll probably be one of your education's most valuable aspects! Advocate for having dedicated sessions with a diverse range of industry members. No matter whether these sessions are done in person or online, they're an excellent chance to hear from someone who's already working and can provide you with insights from different perspectives. Companies are usually happy to support education and will allow their employees to take time for these extra activities. One piece of advice for these meetings: don't be shy! Ask questions. Even if you think your question might be stupid, I guarantee you two things: (1) several classmates would probably like to know the same thing, so you're doing them a favour. (2) For the speaker, receiving some questions after a talk feels way better than looking at a bunch of silent faces.

One last thing: please don't fall into the trap of ignoring horizontal networking. What does this mean? It refers to the level of seniority of those you're trying to connect with. Please avoid trying to suck up to "important" people or collecting impressive business cards while ignoring everyone else. That doesn't mean you shouldn't converse with leaders, founders, and other senior positions – but you should engage with people, not positions. My group of peers has helped keep me sane during my time in the industry so far, and I'd highly encourage you to focus on that in your networking journey. People in a similar professional stage as you can become valuable sounding boards. You can lift each other up, support the group, share knowledge, talk about your experiences, gather feedback, and embark on the industry journey together. And if you're fortunate, some of them also make incredible personal friends.

Regardless of who you're trying to connect with, be authentic. Don't try to sell an idea of yourself or be someone you think people might like. Instead, be yourself and bond with people over similar hobbies, convictions, and passions.

If you think you just need a bit more information to mentally prepare yourself for all that human interaction, worry not. The internet contains articles and how-tos for newcomers and seasoned developers alike. Please just do yourself a favour and steer clear of anyone telling you that you have to change everything about yourself to make *valuable* contacts. Instead, focus on the human factor. For example, journalist Marie Dealessandri wrote a great article about networking and went into details about intentionality, staying true to yourself, and maintaining connections after the initial contact. If you're eager to dive deeper into networking, check it out.[6] Just remember that networking is only as scary as you allow it to be, and it's even more about what you can do for the other person than vice-versa. A lot of people in this industry are genuine, caring, and interesting human beings. Connect with some of them in ways that feel comfortable for you, and I'm sure it will enrich not only your career but your life in general.

NOTES

1. In RPG terms, this means optimising your skill tree for best possible results.
2. You can get started with the following sites: Hitmarker (hitmarker.net/jobs), Remote Game Jobs (remotegamejobs.com), Game Jobs Direct (gamesjobsdirect.com) and Game Dev Jobs (gamedevjobs.com).
3. One great source is Community Club's repository of community salaries (community.club/salaries).
4. Go here and waste an entire weekend browsing comparisons: https://www.numbeo.com/cost-of-living/.
5. IGDA stands for International Game Developers Association. You can find more information about their local chapters here: https://igda.org/chapters.
6. Marie Dealessandri (April 5, 2022): "Tips for intentional and healthy networking", https://www.gamesindustry.biz/tips-for-intentional-and-healthy-networking-gdc-2022.

You Have Found *The One*™ *What Now?*

5

Keep calm and keep your wits about you. It's tempting to hastily submit your resume and a standard cover letter out of fear that the listing might vanish immediately. But rein it in and take a deep breath. If the listing is outstanding, it deserves more attention than a 2 a.m. panic submission. Of course, you should act soon to ensure they don't end the hiring process. But now is the time to sit down and tailor your documents to the role to intrigue the hiring managers enough to invite you for an interview.

5.1 A CLOSER LOOK AT RESUMES

Now's the time to tell you why job listings can be your best friend on the job hunt. But first, we need to talk about the purpose of a resume. It might be the only thing a hiring manager looks at before adding your application to the "yes" or "no" pile. Some companies let machines decide where you land. Technical or formatting errors might put you on the rejection pile before anyone has even read a word you've written. It's exceptionally harsh but the reality is that people involved in hiring usually receive a lot of applications. They need a first selective layer to manage the number of applications so they can consider the remaining ones adequately. The most important task for you is to get through this initial selection. Here's where the resume comes in. An experienced professional needs less than 30 seconds to scan it and decide if you should be contacted. Make these seconds count! They've already told you how, and you most likely missed it.

DOI: 10.1201/9781003310488-5

Job listings result from people dreaming up the perfect candidate. Thus, they're the ideal blueprint for your resume. Remember: there are multiple approaches to creating your resume, and I encourage you to check different strategies. All I can do is tell you what has worked for me and my network in the past.

As basic as it sounds, when I write a resume, I copy and paste the entire listing into a blank document and then condense it sentence by sentence by removing all the fluff until only the requirements and the job description are left. Then, I add a new row for every task or required skill, and highlight the elements I consider most important. For every line, I think about something I did that proves the skill and write it next to the original text, and phrase it in a way that includes keywords from the original. Of course, it cannot sound like a blatant copy, but it should make recruiters notice the applicability to their listing. Once nothing essential is missing, I delete all the remaining lines from the job listing.

Give it a go. Notice any patterns? You're looking at the core aspects that recruiters will scan your resume for. You should now be looking at your distilled experience and skills, which are fine-tuned to this specific position. Congratulations for finishing the hardest part.

Now, you can use any resume template you find online and merge it carefully with your document. Make it easy to see your skills at first glance. There are different camps, but I'm adamantly on the side of, "fit your resume on a single page." In my opinion, having two pages invites you to write too much fluff that dilutes the core of your resume. There's always fat to trim. Use the whole page, work with columns, eliminate white spaces – and think twice about every word you include.

5.2 ABOUT COVER LETTERS AND PORTFOLIOS

There's a lot of discourse around cover letters. For many, it's probably the most hated part of the application process. I've seen people call cover letters examples of useless self-promotion. On the other end of the spectrum, some claim only a proper cover letter reveals whether an applicant paid attention to the job listing and has what it takes to excel in an interview. I honestly don't have strong feelings about them. Do I enjoy writing them? No. Is it the worst thing you could ask me to do? Also no. They're often a necessary evil of job-hunting that – at least for me – wouldn't be a reason to skip on an otherwise great opportunity.

So how do you write one? Don't get your information on this topic from this book alone. I've seen numerous applications and cover letters over the years, but I'm not a recruiter. What I can do is share some knowledge of what I picked up, what people have told me, and what makes me perk up and pay closer attention when I read them. One crucial thing: don't just reuse the same cover letter for every job. Instead, tailor the cover letter to the specific job you're applying for. This might seem like a giant waste of time; how different can they be anyway? Very different, I'm afraid. If you read dozens or hundreds of cover letters, you'll know who read the listing and browsed the company website thoroughly – and who pasted their contact details into a pre-made template. Receiving a cover letter explicitly addressed to other AAA studios is something I've witnessed more than once. Trust me: it's hard to come back from that.

So, what does tailoring mean? Some companies will include pointers about what they want to know from you. If they're extending this helpful branch, take it. Even if there's no further information about the cover letter, there are some tips you can follow. Be concise, and don't lose yourself in empty phrases. Aim for around four or five paragraphs in which you talk about the following things: your years of experience and in what roles, your most applicable projects and things you learned that can help you in the new job, what skills you're bringing to the table, and why you want to apply them to this role. Be specific without losing yourself in the details. Pick a few requested skills from the job listing that you believe you're particularly good at, and weave your cover letter around those. You don't have to tell them everything there's to know about you. Just make them so curious that they simply have to invite you to an interview. Don't waste your limited space for explaining why you want to leave your previous employer or share negativity. If it doesn't serve to highlight your skills and how you could benefit the company, it has no place. That also means you shouldn't discuss projects, work experience, or transferrable skills without connection to the new role. Instead, use the cover letter to complement your resume. If there's something in your resume that you feel deserves more attention, pick it up in the cover letter. When writing about duties, fill them with life. Instead of writing, "managed the community for x," write something like, "grew the community to x active members by doing y." In the best-case scenario, crafting a great cover letter can help you think through the interview process, verbalise your motivation for the role, and how your skills are applicable.

One subject people rarely discuss about CM applications is portfolios. It might initially feel awkward to think about it. For instance, my first reaction to the idea was: *what am I even creating to put into one?* I haven't heard of a job listing for CMs that mandates applicants to provide a portfolio, but having a collection of the coolest things you've done can really help. Curating a space for yourself where you add personal highlights also helps battling imposter syndrome, should you suffer from it. If you create a portfolio, remember three things: (1) don't break any NDAs. (2) Be mindful of what you share and keep potential risks to yourself in mind. Please don't share private contact information on there, and don't include pictures that might give away where you live.[1] (3) It's your space. You decide what's important and what it looks like. Did you have a job you think didn't contribute to your growth? Don't mention it! Are you proud of performing on stage in front of a live audience? Include it! Show personality and intrigue your potential employers. Treat your portfolio as a living organism. Whenever you finish working on something terrific or a project that showcases a different skill, add it to your portfolio. *But what if I have nothing to add to my portfolio because I haven't worked yet*? I hear you. Keep it minimalistic. Make it a one-pager with a short description of yourself that goes into one or two key interests or facts that make you stand out from other applicants. Include some of your favourite games or genres – since you want to work in gaming, you should give people an idea about your preferences. Next, list your primary skills and in what role you'd like to apply them. If you feel comfortable with it, add a picture of yourself that, ideally, shows your personality. It doesn't have to be formal, as long as you wouldn't be embarrassed knowing that your future boss or clients have seen it. As a finishing touch, add links to your social platforms and consider adding a contact form so people can reach out. If you already have any professional experience under your belt, include details. Split it into clear sections that highlight different experiences and projects. What have you done in each project? Were you responsible for writing copy? Did you communicate feedback? Organise an event? Host meetings? Describe the goals for each task and how you reached them. If any of this information can be found online, I'd link to it to provide references. Once you're happy with your portfolio, include a link to the hosted[2] version on your resume next to other contact details.

There's no denying that a portfolio is a lot of additional work, but once a recruiter is already interested in you, having one might tip the scales in your favour. I'd also consider doing it for yourself. Working in communication can feel very intangible. Gathering all your skills and projects in one space can remind you of your growth and the goals you're working towards.

5.3 "WE DO NOT LIE" AND OTHER TIPS

You're about to submit your application. Pause for a moment. Ask yourself: is everything in your application true? Did you mention your fluent French, when really the last time you spoke the language was during a vacation over a decade ago? Or maybe you've exaggerated your previous responsibilities? Do yourself a favour and be honest. Hiring managers are adept at asking questions and probing your skills. Even if the remainder of the conversation went well, an uncovered lie in the application could risk its whole success. If you're lying about something like this, it raises the question of what else you're willing to lie about. Don't sabotage your own success; just be honest. It's all too easy to meet a hiring manager who might ask a follow-up question that will trip you up.

Do your research on the company and its games. Read up on the most critical beats from the company's history. One thing that could set you apart is looking closely at their communication. When do they start their campaigns, and how do they choose to communicate on social media? Are there platforms you think would be a great fit but aren't used by the company? Don't criticise all their work during your interview, especially not without being asked for feedback. However, if your interviewer asks what you would change about their current communication strategy, delivering a thoughtful response might make the difference.

5.4 NEW MISSION ACCEPTED: WORKING IN COMMUNITY MANAGEMENT

Bo de Vries

Please note: my professional experience is solely with larger game companies in Europe. This chapter provides personal insights and is not a reflection of my past or current employer.

Back in 2011, a company approached me to have a chat about a role they were hiring for. "Community Manager?" I thought, "What in the world does that even mean?" I was fresh out of university, in my first media job, and commuted three hours a day feeling like a small-town big shot. I loved working in TV, but videogames were my true passion – I just had no idea there were jobs out there that would suit my degree or skill set.

Reading the job listing was a huge revelation: communication skills? Social media knowledge? Engaging with fans? Attending gaming events? I researched the company all night to figure out what exactly this opportunity was, and realised that this Community Manager job might be the answer that my soul-searching post-grad self had been looking for.

Fast forward over a decade later… I'm now in the humbling position where I get to meet, mentor, and hire the next generation of talent in this discipline, and despite how straightforwardly I just described the start of my journey into the industry, it can still be tricky or overwhelming to know where to begin. By sharing some insights from someone who's been a Hiring Manager for a few years, I hope you'll feel more informed about what the hiring process for Community roles can look like, as well as more reassured that finding the right role for you is not as daunting as it may seem!

WE'RE HIRING – NOW WHAT?

The hiring process starts by asking a lot of questions to figure out who exactly we're going to be looking for. What big "beats" are coming up for the game or the studio and are we equipped for those? Are we growing a Twitch channel and should we therefore be looking for someone with presenting or streaming experience? Do we have a lot of seniors who are ready and able to train juniors? Or maybe we need a generalist, someone who is equally at home in any specialisation and able to help out with a lot of projects? The answers to these questions help form a profile, which will then be used to create the job listing.

Once a job goes live on the company website and LinkedIn, it's time to amplify! We'll post links on the company social channels and recruiters will reach out to industry folk to spread awareness of new openings. Community listings usually stay active for a week or two; such roles are often in high demand as there's a lot of crossover with other disciplines like Customer Support, Communications, PR, or content creation – making it a diverse and popular point of entry into the game industry.

Community roles can easily get 50+ applications in just a few days, and as a Hiring Manager, I'd likely select around ten people for an initial interview. This keeps the candidate pool to those with the strongest potential and avoids the interview process becoming too time-consuming for internal team members who are also part of interview rounds. It's always good to be ready with an up-to-date CV and a base cover letter if you're actively looking for jobs, so you can be part of the first batch of applications for a role.

SIDE QUEST: LANDING AN INTERVIEW WITH A STAND-OUT APPLICATION

There's a couple of important things I'd look at when deciding who proceeds to interviews. First of all, did you follow the application instructions? Is there a cover letter if that was requested? Is the application written in English (you'd be surprised how many people submit in a company's local language despite the listing specifying English as the main language!)? Are there any obvious copy errors (if you use a base cover letter, please be sure to remove another company's or hiring manager's name from your opening …)? Have a friend check your resume before submitting, double check the details, and just be sure to follow the application instructions to a T!

Next, how does your experience match the outlined qualifications in the job listing? How many years have you worked in the field, or, for junior roles, do you have a relevant degree or extracurricular activity that shows your relevance to the role (i.e., volunteer modding experience or customer-facing jobs like retail match well with CM skills). It's fine to stick to linear CV conventions, but it might be smart to highlight your most relevant experience clearly for the reader.

Here's a few things that usually stand out to me when going through CVs:

- Use design to your advantage! Colour, shapes, or section bars can help certain areas stand out as they naturally draw the eye there; putting important information there that aligns with the job description is really helpful. If you're not feeling super creative, there are loads of nice templates online that will save you from having to design something from scratch.
- Add some personality! I love reading about what makes you YOU, like hobbies or volunteering experience; it paints a picture about you as a person and how you would fit in with your team members. Add links to relevant work as well, like a livestream or fan art channel.
- There's nothing wrong with a bit of topical humour; one of my favourite CVs ever had headers like "Quests Completed" and "Easter Eggs" to describe experience and personality!

Be mindful of being too silly as some jokes or design choices simply don't translate and would distract a reader from your actual qualifications. Take that extra step to update your CV so it links directly to the job's requirements, don't be afraid to add a nice design, and definitely get someone to proofread your materials before you send it!

Motivation and being passionate about the game or company you'd represent as a Community professional are incredibly important; a cover letter (or portfolio, if requested) is a great way to emphasise that passion with personal insight on a relevant experience that made you want to work in games. It's wonderful to read what a game means to you, and how you would translate that love or passion to your day-to-day job; it's also a great conversation starter when you land that first interview. I've read a multitude of fascinating stories about people's favourite games and their impact, but my all-time favourite cover letter was a beautiful story about how playing games together with a parent deepened their bond, inspiring that person to work in games so they could share that joy with others – a true tear-jerker!

Finally, a Community Hiring Manager will always visit your social media profiles. This is an important check for any Community or consumer-facing role! As a CM, you'll represent a brand, a company, and the work of your colleagues – so being a decent human being, online and offline, is a necessity.

MISSION UPDATE: PREPARE, PREPARE, PREPARE!

Congrats, you've got an interview! Now is the time to research the company and create a list of questions you'd like to ask the team. It's likely that the first person you'll speak to is the (in-house) recruiter for the role, who'll ask you about why you've applied, your salary expectations, and discuss potential relocation. They'll also tell you a bit more about the company and gauge you as a person: are you going to be a good fit for the team? This chat gives a company an informed picture of your initial expectations and ability to follow up on any of your questions.

This is your time to be authentic and upfront about your needs – which is why the prior research and preparation are key! Be informed about your worth; research what similar positions in your country earn as this gives you a good indication when asked about salary expectations. If the job is not remote and you are being asked to relocate or commute, look into the cost of living of that city to get a better understanding of what you'll require to live comfortably. If you're working from home or freelancing, have an overview at hand of your monthly spendings or required equipment.

Sometimes this initial bit is done via email, so your first interview is actually with the Hiring Manager or some team members. Though chatting to multiple people may seem overwhelming, it's quite standard – it allows the team to take (and compare) notes, see how you get on with multiple team members, and help each other answer your questions as well. A first interview should be about getting to know you, talking more in-depth about the role's responsibilities, and giving you an opportunity to ask questions to the team.

By the way, it's okay to be nervous, and to mention that! I always do my best to break the ice in the beginning, to make you feel safe and comfortable, and to let you talk freely about your experiences. I usually also ask whether you would prefer to start by talking about yourself or if it would help if I start with a little outline of the role and the company. Allowing you to have ownership of your interview is really important, as it gives you the chance to ease into the flow of the conversation and helps calm those nerves. If at any point you get overwhelmed or lose track of your thoughts: stop, breathe, and just acknowledge that you're nervous or you'll revisit that thought later. Remember that you're talking to another human being who's been in your position, and who understands that you might be feeling the pressure.

Among those normal nerves, interview excitement, and all the new information that will have your head spinning, it can be easy to forget all that's been discussed in an interview. I'd advise you to keep notes throughout to help you remember how you felt afterwards. Ask yourself if the interview felt genuine? Were the people friendly and welcoming? Did you get all your questions answered? It's important to remember throughout the process that you also have to get a good feeling from your potential future team and company!

Writing down details before and after each interview has been my lifesaver on many occasions, and if there's anything that's still unclear: follow up with questions! You can always reach out to the appropriate contact person to ask for clarifications or additional details. It's easy to worry about coming across as "too demanding" but ultimately this is a big step in your life that requires and deserves full support from a future employer.

SKILL TREE COMPLETED

During interviews, other than talking about who you are, there'll be a skill check based on the job requirements. There are hard and soft skills: they have varying definitions but it really comes down to hard skills being knowledge-based and measurable, whereas soft skills are more like personality traits.

Some Community hard skill examples would be:

- Time management, because we often work to specific campaign deadlines and own a variety of tasks. An interview question could be: "Can you give an example of a project where you had to manage multiple tasks simultaneously or work to a hard deadline?"

- Data analysis, because having a basic understanding of social media analytics is an incredible source of insight for any CM in terms of player sentiment or player retention, as well as helping you communicate challenges or success to stakeholders and internal developers. An example question could be: "Have you run a successful campaign on [insert relevant social channel] before, and how was that success quantified?" or "How do you report on your community analytics in your current role?"
- Content creation, as a means to communicate and engage with the players. For example: "Take us through a weekly social plan" or "What type of social media content do you think would resonate well with the community?"

Soft skills are gauged through your responses and the connection you have with the team. Some examples would be:

- Empathy, because as a CM, it's important to be able to relate to players and kindly communicate with them, such as "How would you address a negative player about [topic]?"
- Self-awareness, or emotional maturity, is important in this role because you need to have strong boundaries when you're active on social media or community forums. An example question could be "Describe a recent stressful moment you experienced at work and how you dealt with that professionally."
- Creativity, where we would mostly look at your ability to come up with fresh ideas to keep the fans engaged, like "Tell us about a community activation or content you came up with that positively impacted or engaged players."

It's important to note here that these questions highly depend on seniority – I wouldn't ask a more junior candidate too many in-depth things, but instead focus more on their interests and potential future growth, whereas a more senior candidate would be expected to give lots of examples of previous experiences and contributions.

MISSION COMPLETE: CAREER LAUNCH CONFIRMED!

Ultimately, the Hiring Manager decides on the most successful candidate and the recruiter will then present an offer; this should include a salary range, start date, and contract length at the very least. Before signing, be sure to ask any final questions, negotiate your terms, and weigh up your options. Remember that it's equally important that you feel comfortable joining the team, feel informed about what you're signing, and clearly define what the company expects from you, and what you can expect from the company. Hopefully with some of the advice from this chapter and the rest of this book, you'll have a great offer in front of you.

Community Management is a really exciting and ever-evolving discipline that offers a great career opportunity for those looking to build connections with players, create engaging content for social channels, and represent the work of talented developers. It's already so different compared to when I started over 10 years ago, with sub-disciplines emerging in Social Media, Content Creation, Moderation, and more. Companies continue to better understand the huge value of such roles, especially after a global pandemic, where people searched for human connection, immersive stories, and escapism through video games – and Community professionals played a vital role in fostering those connections.

5.5 WHAT IS AN NDA?

The games industry really loves NDAs. That's short for non-disclosure agreement – a legally binding document you have to sign before you can be entrusted with any confidential information. Most hiring processes include this, so don't be alarmed if you're sent one. If the interviewer needs to talk to you about upcoming tasks or projects, that's already reason enough for them to request one. Its purpose is to prohibit you from sharing sensitive information you learned during the interview or on the job. Otherwise, nothing (apart from your professionalism) could stop you from sharing details on social media that might damage the company's plans. Usually, you'll receive the NDA together with the invitation for the first interview or right before it. However, as with every legal document, please read it before signing! Check the consequences of an NDA breach – and what's considered one. The scope of protected information shouldn't include things already publicly available. Some companies also require you to submit tasks or work samples; be wary if the NDA contains clauses that would transfer all rights to your work during the recruitment phase to the company. Don't feel shy to ask for more details.

Gladly, many NDAs today instead include a clause that the company may only use submitted materials for the hiring process. I believe there's no proper reason for the opposite to be the case before you've even signed on for the job. In most cases, though, there's absolutely no reason to be concerned about an NDA if you do your due diligence.

5.6 WHAT TO DO IF YOU GET REJECTED

If you're not the absolute exception, you'll experience rejections in your professional career. Please prepare yourself to receive an email thanking you for your application, but they ultimately went with another candidate. Or even more gruesome, you'll pour sweat and tears into your application, tell your closest friends how excited you are, send it off, and ... nothing. Not even an automated email. Until one day you learn from Twitter that they hired someone else. I won't pretend it doesn't hurt, but there are ways to turn it into a less painful experience.

But first things first. If you weren't hired for the position, don't be the person who jumps on social media and complains about not getting the job.[3] This should go without saying, but don't insult employees or the company. If

The gaming industry is incredibly small and difficult to get in to. Do not get disheartened if you are rejected frequently, it truly happens to everyone getting into the industry. Take the time to keep honing your own skills, learn from people that work in the industry already through social media, panels and talks, and keep trying!

————— CHANTE GOODMAN

> *It can be a long road of rejection. But start by doing side projects that exhibit your skill and put in the work for yourself or friends. Never work for free though. Your time is precious.*
>
> ———— COLE

you still want to work in the industry, this behaviour can seriously damage your prospects, especially in a communication position. Instead, remind yourself that there are still humans involved who had to make a hard decision. If you received a rejection email, send back a simple email thanking them for their time and wishing them all the best with the new colleague. And, of course, you're happy to hear back from them should new opportunities arise. Should you see the newly hired person on social media happily announcing the role you wanted, repeat after me: that's great! Someone got a job and is sharing the excitement. Congratulating that person can go a long way towards building relationships and internalising that you'll be their colleague or peer one day.

As a mid-term step, think about the why. I'm not inviting you to obsess over your imagined shortcomings – but to look at the situation rationally. Were your documents free of mistakes and in line with what was asked for? It might be worth sharing with a friend or family member since developing a distorted view of your writing and design is easy. If you can't spot any issues with your application and were already in the interview stage, do you think you adequately responded to all the questions? Try recreating the conversation. Write down the questions and answers and check online how you might respond better.

Last, maybe it has nothing to do with you or your qualifications at all. Hiring managers are humans, and processes are rarely perfect. There'll always be subjective elements. Maybe the successful candidate offered an earlier possible starting date. Perhaps that person possesses a skill not asked for in the listing but that the company secretly needs. Or maybe they were already in conversation with their dream candidate and were required to post the listing to follow internal guidelines. There are dozens of reasons not to turn a rejection of an application into one for yourself.

Most importantly: try again. Don't be discouraged if you don't get the job the first time. Apply for every role you see yourself in. If a company that rejected you publishes another suitable position, apply again! Show them how much you want it. It takes resilience to land a job in this field in the current job market, and you deserve to be a part of it. I urge you to keep believing that.

NOTES

1. This might sound self-explanatory, but I've seen people share their home address on their portfolio website, and I don't want you to have any nasty surprises.
2. At the time of writing this, I'd recommend looking into WordPress as it provides great service for a small price. This information might be outdated at some point but searching for it with "alternative" should help.
3. One big exception: If you witnessed clear misdemeanor during your interview, feel free to file a complaint about it (or write a scathing review on Glassdoor). Count your blessings this came out in the interview before you signed any contracts.

First Day on the Job

6

6.1 SETTLING IN

Congratulations! I bet you're incredibly excited but also somewhat over-whelmed. What should you start with? Who are all these people? Settling into any new position can feel daunting, but good employers have onboarding processes to alleviate that. Depending on the size of your new professional home, onboarding can take different shapes. Bigger companies might have you run through a full-day session, presenting you with everything from legal guidelines and game design documents to event policies. In other companies, it could be just you and your lead discussing the most important things. This is the time to be curious and take lots of notes. You're here to learn, and good teams will reward that attitude. Ask for recordings of previous meetings or other documentation to get as much information about your new job as possible. If you're looking for a condensed list of tips for your first day, Figure 6.1 shows some of my peers' recommendations.

6.2 FINDING A SPOT IN YOUR TEAM

I hope you're not joining the company in the busiest period of the year. Spending the whole first week working is not the most valuable thing you can do for yourself. While I fully understand the impulse to prove yourself as soon as your account has been set up by IT, rein it in. Remind yourself that your new employer hired you for a reason. Instead of proving what a highly productive workhorse you are, get to know the people you'll work with. Game development is a collaborative effort, and that extends to community management. Nowadays, my approach would be quite straightforward: I'd schedule individual meetings with every team member and introduce

48

DOI: 10.1201/9781003310488-6

FIGURE 6.1   Tips for your first day from experienced CMs.

myself in a casual conversation. I'd ask for recommendations about who else I should speak with from outside our team and then schedule more meetings. My primary goal would be to better understand the people I'll spend so much time with. However, I know what you might be thinking: "Never ever!" Some years ago, there was no scenario in which I'd have proactively set up dozens of calls with strangers. If you feel confident enough already to do this on your first job, I'm amazed and encourage you to try it. If not, feel comforted that you'll probably gain the necessary confidence over the years.

So, what would I recommend if you want to connect with teammates but don't know how?

It highly depends on how comfortable you feel in conversations. I hate small talk. Not in one of these highbrow ways of feeling *above* it; I simply get extremely anxious and physically uncomfortable at the thought of silence. At least it used to be this way. I found two anchors for conversations that prevent me from turning into a sweaty mess: passion and purpose. What does this mean? Try connecting with your colleagues either about things you genuinely care about or for a practical reason. For the former, consider writing a short introduction that includes your favourite hobbies, games, books, movies, travel destinations, animals, or whatever makes you happy. Write from the heart and before you start getting nervous, hit send. If you're unsure if this is okay, check in with your lead and tell them what you want to do. This way, you're opening the door for your colleagues to contact you about mutual interests. If you're anxious when reaching out to others, I hope this approach helps you.

Since you've already been talking to your lead, ask them who could help you get accustomed to certain tools and processes. This represents my *purpose* anchor. Instead of sitting at your desk alone and going through internal presentations, find knowledgeable people who can spare thirty minutes to walk you through what's most important. Everyone can talk to you about one of their specialties. How does the team organise itself? How are passwords and channels handled?

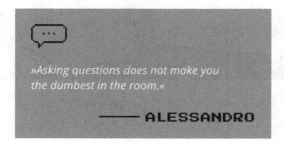

»Asking questions does not make you the dumbest in the room.«

———— ALESSANDRO

What's the communication style on social media? Nothing beats talking to an experienced person who can answer your questions. As a nice side effect, you're getting to know more team members! Make sure to also be in close contact with your lead. What are their primary goals? What bothers them? Get a good idea of your lead's needs and align your upcoming projects accordingly.

A week or two passes, and you're slowly settling in. You recognise most names – maybe you're already exchanging memes with someone – now, just keep going! See if there are projects that allow you to collaborate with team members; when people share accomplishments at work, take a minute to congratulate them. If it's something you'd love to be able to do one day, ask if they have time to sit down and tell you how they achieved it. I sincerely hope you've found a team of kind people who are generous with their knowledge and time.

6.3 USEFUL TOOLS AND STRATEGIES

What tools you'll be working with depends on your new company. Are you faced with 20 internal applications for everything from looking up an asset to booking a day off? Or did you get your work laptop with a freeware license to a chat app and nothing else? I've heard examples of everything between those two extremes. You'll be fine as long as you get acquainted with whatever is at your disposal and are smart about your needs.

Wondering what those needs are? I separate them into three categories: dealing with yourself, dealing with the company, and dealing with the outside world. Since tools are there to serve people, not vice versa, focus on the vital ones. Master the basics and expand once you feel confident; you don't have to go too broad at the beginning. I'll start with one of my non-negotiables: become best friends with your calendar, and learn how to set work hours, mark yourself absent, and create blockers for deep work. Set these boundaries early on. Not only will it help you with the stress of handling too many things simultaneously, but it will also increase your productivity. Just imagine having regular blockers that give you two hours of uninterrupted time – notifications off, no distractions. That's when you can finally get cracking on that pitch you've been itching to work on!

Second on the list of non-negotiables is a good task management tool. You can use the native one integrated into email clients like Google Tasks, Kanban boards such as Trello, or software like Notion. Find one that works for you, and then be as thorough as possible in keeping track of your tasks and allocating priority to them. For me, next to your emails, this covers the main aspects of managing yourself at work at the beginning of your journey.

How you are expected to interact with other members of your company will most likely be part of your onboarding. For more complex apps, you should receive individual training sessions. But what's immediately necessary? Just a few things, actually. Focus on the most practical applications for your work life and figure out how to do those things. Think about: how do you communicate with your team members? How do you share community feedback with others in your company? Do you use Jira? Spreadsheets? Setting these up should be one of your earliest priorities. Furthermore, you need to understand logistics unique to your company, such as: how to apply for paid time off and sick leave, register worked overtime hours, get a graphic asset, or a contract for working with a community ambassador. In the end, it's similar to a game; just like how you don't get every mechanic thrown at you all at once but are given the time to learn them – this is how you should treat your learning journey with internal tools.

Whatever your company uses to deal with the outside world, get a solid grasp of it fast. You'll likely use a content management system (CMS) to publish blog posts or website articles. Learn how this works before you need to post an important message. I could tell you some – NDA'd – nightmare stories of what can go wrong if you don't know which website it posts to when you hit publish. Get acquainted with all platforms you communicate on, whether it's Steam, Facebook, TikTok, Discord, or others. You're probably familiar with most of them, but remember that many of them have *business* or *developer tools* that differ from the standard version.

6.4 UNDERSTANDING THE BEHEMOTH THAT IS A GAME STUDIO

Making games requires a lot of extremely specialised people. Whether it's a handful, a hundred, or a couple of thousand, they'll deal with topics you know nothing about. You'll encounter barriers when creating projects because you won't realise that a particular department needs to weigh in. Instead of letting it overwhelm you, embrace it. This still happens to me after years of working in the same place; it keeps me on my toes, and I love it. If you don't understand something, ask. People at game studios love talking about their work. This curiosity will help you learn more about the industry, your company, its games, and your colleagues. It expands your internal network of people and can give you fresh ideas. Slowly, you'll get the hang of it by asking questions and drawing mind maps of the overall studio. It'll probably take years, but that's okay. We're all still doing it one way or another.

Because of the many differences across the industry, it's impossible for me to prepare you for every possible setup at your company. Just like community management isn't standardised, neither are company structures and departmental naming conventions. At first, you'll most likely be in closer contact with colleagues from the marketing department, including brand, digital, and email marketing, copywriting, influencer, social media, product management, public relations, and user acquisition.[1] We could spend a lot of time discussing what else belongs on this list, but my main intention is to show you the diversity of this one department alone. Sooner rather than later, you'll probably collaborate with the legal, finance, or business development teams for contests, partnerships, or budget plans. I recommend starting with these teams as you begin your journey in getting to know the company. Should you be working in a small company where you combine several positions, this makes it even more vital for you to connect with the others around you to ease the burden on your shoulders.

NOTE

1. Hitmarker. "The complete list of gaming jobs." July 4, 2022. hitmarker.net/career-advice/the-complete-list-of-gaming-jobs.

How to Community Manage

7

You made it! You've found a job, settled into your team, and are beginning to understand the differences between departments. Now it's time to get to work. What exactly you're facing depends on the size of your team, the kind of game you're working on, what platforms and age range it targets, whether it already has an established community, and much more. Regardless of any of that, all of us CMs share one thing: we're the bridge builders between our players and our development teams.

We translate the information our studios want to communicate into something the community understands and cares about. On the flip side, we gather the community's sentiment about company announcements and condense it into actionable feedback for the developers. Sounds simple enough, doesn't it? So, let's get started!

In most cases, your company won't hire you as a novice without any support system to learn from. That's why you can ask your colleagues how they structure their workday, what their priorities are, and what documents you should stay on top of. If a company has no communications department, and you would be their first hire, we're likely talking about small independent teams looking for someone to handle their social media channels or manage a surprisingly successful early access release. In this case, please ensure you can grow with the team – and aren't expected to clean up years of ignored communication in one month.

The following chapters introduce different aspects of this role – from creating a strategy to actively including your community or celebrating your devs. But let's start with some essential first-aid tips for the day after you've done all your 1:1s and read all the onboarding documents. If you don't know where to start, ask yourself the following three questions and let the answers guide you. Everything else is the second step.

DOI: 10.1201/9781003310488-7

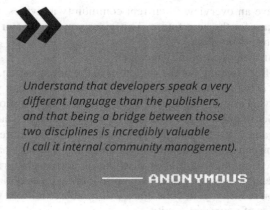

> Understand that developers speak a very
> different language than the publishers,
> and that being a bridge between those
> two disciplines is incredibly valuable
> (I call it internal community management).
>
> ———— ANONYMOUS

1. What have we committed to so far?

The sad reality is that you're unlikely to join a project early enough to be working from a blank slate. Even if you're the first CM, the team has most likely previously communicated things to the outside world, tried managing platforms, or made promises for the future. That's totally fine. Now, it's your job to process all of that. The last thing you want is to start your community job by breaking with everything the community is used to. To keep track, make a big list by writing down everything that helps you understand things better. Here are some starter questions: are your games released on a storefront? If yes, does this storefront have community features like forums or reviews? Can you publish news and updates for your game? Are there any existing social media channels for the game or company? If yes, are there any (semi-) running community projects? Even if it's something as small as scheduling a screenshot for every Saturday, write it down. If you don't want to continue projects, having a complete overview allows you to make educated decisions once you start creating a strategy. Are there other ways for the community to submit feedback? Is there any process to inform developers about community sentiment? Include any goals or plans shared with you during your initial conversations with your team. Maybe they shared that they'd love to attend an event or set up a streaming format; perhaps the team promised they'd start a weekly Q&A on their Discord. You know what I'll say: it goes onto the list. Once you've gathered all this information, you have an overview of current community activities, promises, and plans for the near future. This gives you a great starting point for things to work on.

2. Who are your community members?

After mapping out the responses to the first question, we know how it *is* but not necessarily how it *should be*. How can you determine what you should double down on and what you should phase out? Get to know your community by researching the audience of your games. It's time to put your data hat on! The more information you can find, the better. Check internally if anyone has already gathered numbers on player distribution across platforms, genre preferences, ages, or gender. If you're joining an established team and you're lucky, your colleagues will be able to tell you the demographics of your community.

If you're the first person in the company to handle community management, or your colleagues have mainly acted on gut feeling, it's time to work with the data you've gathered. Cluster it into different categories, and based on that, imagine examples of the people this could represent. One data cluster might remind you of high school students playing games on their phones with their friends while waiting for the bus in the morning. Another might be middle-aged workers wanting to disconnect for 20 minutes on their way back from the office. Remember that you're not creating a community for yourself. Communicating without knowing who you're talking to makes it challenging to successfully convey your intended message. The example hopefully illustrates the necessity of distinct approaches when talking to players and creating content that speaks to them. You may have already heard someone talk in marketing lingo about *creating personas,* and what I'm laying out here is a highly simplified explanation of that. Crucially, audiences can vary significantly if your company has more than one game. It takes time but analyse the audience for every game independently.

Now you hopefully have a better understanding of the different people that form your community. The second step is figuring out how these groups interact with your game. Do they seek out Steam forums to ask for help? Are they creating community wikis or post their creations on Instagram? Or – do they play your game and don't engage with the community at all? For the last category, aim to create proper onboarding – which I'll describe in the strategy section. For the others, understand why they use each platform. Are they using it because you're not offering a valuable solution for their needs? They may ask a lot of questions on Steam because there's no place to ask you directly. Aim to offer a solution for that. Maybe your company has set up a channel on a certain platform, but most of your community uses another. Question why these channels were set up. You may find out that – as is often the case – people in your company made them because they followed a template of how to do it without understanding that different communities have varying needs and preferences. It's your responsibility to figure out the best use of company resources. If you find a misalignment between your data and the company's behaviour, equip yourself with proper arguments and offer a solution. It can be as simple as opening a YouTube or Instagram account for a community that doesn't respond well to Twitter posts. There's a statement that's almost a platitude by now: follow your community. If they really enjoy one platform, consider creating a presence there.

What should you do if you haven't released a game yet and there's no information about your community from wishlists or social media followers? Don't worry about it. No matter how big they are now, everyone's been there at some point. I'll get into that later in more detail.

3. Is anything on fire?

The last question you should figure out is whether your community is burning. Of course, this isn't your fault (if you manage to burn down a community within your first two weeks, I'm almost impressed), but it'll be at least partially your responsibility to deal with it. We don't worry about current interior design trends if our house is on fire, we just want the fire gone. Similarly, if your community is in an awful spot, it's probably not the right moment to create a new community strategy from scratch. First, the situation needs to calm down. What does a community fire look like in reality? Your company announced a policy change that breaks with previous strategies and angers its player base. A patch the company thought would fix issues instead introduced new ones, which leads the community to review-bomb your game on Steam or Metacritic. A journalist published an extremely negative article about the company culture, and everything you now post on brand accounts gets flooded with criticism. What's vital for you to understand is that you won't fix things this severe with a simple post on social media and that it doesn't rest on your shoulders alone. After all, you just joined. The company requires a proper plan to turn the sentiment around. Depending on the severity of the issue, the plan needs substantial action to accompany any statements to keep them from being empty words. Likely, you won't be in any position to decide the solutions offered to the community, but you can help inform them. The best way to help is to examine why the community is upset and provide this information to those making the call. Work your way from the initial spark that caused the problem to today. Gather and categorise your company's messages on social media or forums. Why exactly are people upset? Do they offer alternatives that would solve the situation? What are underlying frustrations? Sort everything as objectively as possible and draw conclusions to offer possible fixes. Discuss the next steps with your lead when you're satisfied that your summary is accurate. They might tell you to present it to decision-makers. That's awesome! Remember that part of your job is to translate the needs of your community for the studio. The better the company understands what its community really wants, the more successful it will be in the long run. Try to embrace the challenge. Once the situation is at least partially resolved, you can focus on the groundwork. On top of that, you'll have learned crucial tools to help you navigate problems in the future.

With all the tasks and projects facing you, many factors complicate matters. Broadly speaking, communication and marketing together are a constant balancing act of transparency and tension. You want players to feel well-informed while still making them want more to stay curious about your game. While it might feel tempting to just infodump everything on them – after all, it's what people often claim they want – you'll likely find this isn't as successful in building a community as you'd hoped. I had to learn early on that people often say they want one thing but desire something completely different. You have to read between the lines and separate what people say from the underlying needs they communicate.

There are many reasons why you may not be able to tell them everything the moment they ask for it. You might have already planned how you want to share this info later. Another straightforward explanation is that as a company, you simply don't know the answers yet. A game-breaking bug might not be reproducible despite all the devs scrambling to fix it. Adding one feature to the game might mean cutting two others, and the team is trying to decide what to do. *When will this feature be added*? *Why can you not just fix that bug*? *When is the next content drop coming*? Remember that people aren't asking *you*. It's not about your personal thoughts and estimates. When the community reaches out about your games or the company, you're a brand representative. They'll treat what you say as official statements – yes, even when you say that all thoughts

expressed are your own. Depending on your company's newswor-
thiness, the media might start reporting about messages you left
in forums or responses you've given on Twitter. I've had people
screenshot DMs I've sent in good faith and share them on Reddit.
As such, it's tricky to respond with, "I don't know" or to respond
with formerly undisclosed details. It could show numerous things,
all of which aren't the best look for you or your employer. *As a public representative, you're not informed about something relevant to
your job due to poor internal communication. The developers don't
know what they're doing and are struggling to make it work. The
company doesn't care. The communication team isn't aligned.* All
of these are impressions you should try to avoid. It's your responsibility to help protect the devs so they can focus on their jobs. Don't
throw them under the bus with rushed responses. Sometimes, deals
with partners such as platform holders or publishers require secrecy
about specific dates or features because revealing those is part of a
more extensive campaign. Don't jeopardise that by sharing them on
Discord in a casual Friday conversation.

Other times, you're legally prohibited from saying anything. The
NDA and contract you've signed? Those include provisions that keep
you from disclosing information to third parties. If you work for a
stock-traded company, you must abide by additional rules that concern
sharing business-relevant data. Breaking these can have serious consequences. Finally, there will be a time in your career when you have
to communicate something you disagree with. This doesn't have to be
due to big corporate evil. As I've mentioned, making games requires
teamwork, and teamwork includes reaching decisions through compromise. Sometimes, the compromise doesn't make everyone happy.
More often than not, that person might be you. Some examples include
a change in company policy, game delays, and cutting certain features.
You know your community won't like it, and you may disagree –
but remember that you're responsible for translating your company's
needs to the players, not only the other way around.

All the above means it's sometimes better to say nothing. If
you know something is brewing within your community but cannot disclose details, address concerns by saying that the team is
aware of and investigating the issue. That's why you read this
phrase so often. This may all sound frustrating, but it's your job
to find ways to engage your community as best as possible within
these constraints. Managing to do that well is extremely rewarding,
and it's possible, but it requires empathy, creativity, and a well-
planned community strategy.

7.1 COMING UP WITH A STRATEGY

In an ideal world, fresh CMs won't have to create strategies by themselves but get to learn on the job with leads and mentors. However, it can happen that you'll need to come up with one, so I want to give you some pointers to get you started. I should say the most important thing first: there's no one-size-fits-all strategy that works for every game. You might encounter people in the industry who promise you fool-proof solutions. Don't trust them. You'll likely encounter people asking you to *do what went viral for that other game.* I'm sorry, and I feel you. My goal is to equip you with the necessary knowledge for developing your strategy and making decisions that feel right for you and your community.

Before I go into details: what do I mean by strategy, and why is it important? You should have goals for your game that you want to achieve as a company. As a community team or individual manager, you only have limited resources (workforce, budget, and time) available to achieve these objectives. In straightforward terms, your strategy describes how best to use the resources you have to achieve your desired goal. Ideally, this process should be kicked off with some good old research. Ultimately, you should know what else you're competing with for your audience's time and attention and what elements of your game are its main selling points. Highlight those in your communication. Maybe you're lucky and someone has already created a competitive analysis or an overview of the game's unique features. That's a great starting point you should peruse thoroughly, but it doesn't replace digging into both the game and comparable titles yourself. People look at games differently depending on their priorities and experiences. The crucial element is understanding the community appeal as early as possible, and that's where you come in. Take an honest look at the game and consider the players who might like it. Note everything down with ample space for comments. What are the defining elements of the game that might attract people?

First, and probably most obviously, look at the type of game: is it a racing game, a turn-based strategy, an action role-playing game, or maybe a mashup of several genres? How does the game follow the standards of others in the same bracket, and are there ways in which it modernises or subverts expectations? Look at the community campaigns of the most successful representatives of that category to see what you and the community like and dislike.

Second, does the game belong to an established brand with a fanbase waiting for new adventures, or is it a new intellectual property (IP) offering you a fresh canvas? Similarly, consider the game's setting, as some have avid supporters. From post-apocalypse to Feudal Japan and Lovecraftian horror – certain words attract an audience by their appeal alone, regardless of the genre.

The third aspect requires the most intimate knowledge about the game: what's the main emotion it evokes in the player? Is the game scratching an itch for exploration? Does it invite people to sit back and relax? Are players expected to compete with others? Is the primary goal hoarding dragon scales? Two games can have different mechanics, be set in vastly different environments, and yet make the players feel a similar way. Identify the emotional core of your game and make a list of games that hit a similar spot. How do they activate their communities?

All three of these elements are relevant to your research. Of course, don't copy what other studios are doing. Instead, I want you to use this exercise to properly think through all aspects of the game, get inspired by others, and go beyond the most obvious options.

Once you know what could work for your game, the next step is to think about the tone of voice. If you have a dedicated social media team, they'll have this conversation on their end. Even then, align with them because it should be intertwined with the overall community strategy. Should you be tasked with setting up or taking over social media platforms, the tone can be the first thing to set your channels apart. Even with a well-thought-out publication plan, your potential audience might scroll past your updates if they don't catch their attention and are compelling to read. You wouldn't download a random stock image to promote a release, so don't use cookie-cutter language for the words accompanying it, either. The tone of voice describes the specific way you speak to your audience across your different online representations, such as the character in which you speak, the words you use, and the level of familiarity – including the number of memes and emojis you're comfortable using. There are different schools of thought about whether you should be consistent across all your channels. While there are arguments for sounding the same everywhere – after all, you're the same company, be it on Instagram, LinkedIn, or Tumblr – I think it would be a potential disservice to your audiences and not the best use of your resources. Instead of rigidly following rules you find online, think about what you're trying to achieve and decide based on that. Most likely, you want to reach your identified target audience in an engaging way and, at the same time, properly present your game and company, including its values and characteristics. At this point, you should already have done all your research, so you should know the answers to questions like: who do I want to reach? How do they speak online? What interests them? What characterises my game? What values does our company stand for? To help you get familiar with tone, focus on some critical online messages and try writing as this persona. The more human and less robotic it sounds, the better. This doesn't mean you have to be colloquial. You can still have a human-sounding tone while being more formal. As you can see, I prefer to adapt the tone to the platform. That's mainly due to platforms' different purposes and why people use them. I've grown a professional Tumblr account before, where I happily embraced the purposeful weirdness of that community. At the same time, I've posted the same base message in a friendly neutral voice on Facebook to get the information out to a broader, less-defined audience. It's all about knowing who you're speaking with.

Obviously, the specific kind of game you're trying to communicate and the way of releasing it will significantly influence how to build your strategy. So, let's look at some factors that can make or break the success of your plans.

7.1.1 Existing Versus New Communities

Whether you're inheriting an existing community, can draw upon a similar established community, or have to build one up from scratch, it makes a big difference. All three of these come with different challenges and benefits; if you step into a community that's already well-established, has games or other products on the market, and its own inside jokes, you have to do intense research. How do you spell the names of characters and locations? What jokes work well? What bugs are you allowed to make fun of, and which ones are a thorn in the side of the community? You need to absorb much informal knowledge to be fully welcomed into a community. While you should read up on internal documentation, there's nothing better than observing the community. When I first got my job, I spent my first week diving into the rabbit holes of various community wikis and stalking Facebook groups and subreddits.

On the one hand, this scenario is simpler because you mainly need to manage the current status to reap the fruits of previous labour. Keep people engaged with new activations and informed with updates, and you're mostly golden. However, the challenge here lies in not relying too much on the tried and tested. You have to keep evolving to balance the needs of your loyal core audience and new community members. Hopefully your research helps you come up with fresh takes.

On the other hand, if you're itching to try something new and change how the game is communicated – or simply struggling to get into the vernacular – you may wish for a blank slate. You'll often be brought onto a project that's either been announced or even released. In that case, you're laying the tracks before a moving train. You have to decide upon a direction, tone, and strategy while you lack the time to thoroughly research first. This is overwhelming but also very rewarding if you make it work. Experimentation is key. Try different approaches, iterate, and you will find a tailored way for your new community.

The third case is technically a subgroup of the previous one: building a community for a new IP without pre-existing communities. So far, so similar. However, no rule says you cannot get inspired by other games. Very few games are completely unique. As games draw upon each other, so can communicators draw upon what worked for similar games. When I say similar, I once again refer to a plethora of similarities – from genre and mechanics to overall emotional themes. If you're developing a post-apocalyptic RPG where the player controls a cast of characters, it would be a waste to not learn from games within the genre or those that investigate post-apocalyptic themes. What did their communities react well to? What didn't seem to have worked from your outsider's perspective? Take notes and learn from as many examples as possible. Just make sure to adapt it to your company's game and avoid copying the work of others.

Whether you develop a strategy for a pre-existing or new community, neither is better or necessarily easier than the others. It's also a matter of preference. What's crucial in all three cases is that you work with other departments to keep the messaging as consistent as possible across all external communications.

7.1.2 Different Platforms

Your strategy should differ depending on your release platforms. On average, mobile players have different communicative styles than people who play on Steam. Even then, both are such broad categories that you encounter the full spectrum of games within the PC gaming sphere, from the most core to the most relaxed experiences. Similarly, the stereotype that everyone who plays games on mobile devices is *a casual* (gasp!) has long been debunked, and the portfolio of mobile games today is as vast as on any other platform. So why bring it up? Because players have different expectations and ways to engage with the platforms.

From my – albeit non-representative – experience across several platforms, players on PC are usually more willing to tinker with settings and try a handful of potential solutions before asking for help. Their mobile counterparts expect a game to work without additional hassle. In addition, you'll encounter different contexts for the timing and reasons why people play your game, and you'll have to adapt your communication to reflect your game's control schemes and user interface. Some features might be available on the console version that mobile users cannot access, and touch functionalities that scored well in playtests won't be available to large parts of your audience. Consider all these elements when creating your strategy.

7.1.3 One Size Does Not Fit All

If it hasn't already become apparent, one of my pet peeves is people thinking the job is the same regardless of the game. Don't fall into this trap. Look closely at the content and themes of your game as well as its high-level aspects. If you try to replicate a successful single-player campaign for your multiplayer title, you might soon face dissatisfied players yearning for protection against toxic individuals, clearly communicated balancing fixes, and updates that take their feedback into account. Similarly, drafting a strategy for your mobile game that duplicates popular AAA live service games might sound good on paper – after all, they're both continuously updated games – but could lead to you ignoring the needs and preferences of your core audience. I'm not telling you to ignore trends in other parts of the industry, just make sure to focus on what works for games with similar playstyles to yours. Once you have a good overview, you can make more informed decisions – where to follow industry standards and where to deviate from them. You may need to fight against people urging you to *do what that other company did*. Remember, you're there as an expert for community engagement. It's your job to ensure the strategy is right for *your* game and *your* community.

7.1.4 "Traditional Publishing," Early Access, and More

In many ways, the games industry has become more diverse over the last decades. This also applies to how creators can put their games in front of audiences. For developers, there are probably more ways than ever to publish games, from the more traditional publisher-developer model to creating a Kickstarter campaign or self-publishing on platforms like itch.io. In addition, releasing a full game once it's done is no longer the only option; instead, more games release as early access titles. How your company positions itself in this marketplace is another aspect to consider when creating the community strategy. I cringe whenever I see Kickstarter campaigns or early access titles without full-time community support. Those two probably require successful community management most to thrive. You need to understand the sentiment around your announced plans – and the game's current build – and translate it into actionable feedback for the team. In a way, incorporating community feedback into your final release build is one of the main appeals of early access. As you can imagine, this requires a tailored approach. Your communication has to reinforce two concepts clearly and often: *please give us feedback,* and *we are listening to you*! Set up clear and low-threshold mechanisms for your community to share their insights. This could be in dedicated forum threads, feedback forms, or a special part of your Discord. Make sure people know where to go and have selected spaces where you can gather sentiment – instead of scraping it from various corners of the Internet. Establish something similar internally to ensure your team knows where to find your community sentiment and conclusions. Prioritise issues and wishes according to what the community tells you. Discuss with the dev team how they can include consistent updates to the game that reflect these wishes wherever feasible. Of course, listening to the community is a relevant part of any campaign and not exclusive to these release types. But where the core community work with regular single- or multiplayer launches kicks off with the actual launch, the bulk of the work in Kickstarter or early access starts much, much earlier.

By no means do I claim that this is an all-encompassing checklist for creating your community strategy. However, when you're just starting out and everything is new, it doesn't have to be perfect. It has to be doable. The most important thing is ensuring you understand the following aspects: what do you want to achieve, and what are the smaller objectives on the way? Which steps do you plan to take, and how will you influence community behaviour? How do you make sure the strategy stays relevant? You're already ahead of many people if you can answer these questions. I hope this helps you understand the different elements to shape your plans. Remember, you're not alone and have plenty of resources to pull from and peers to speak to.

7.1.5 HOW TO LIVE, LAUGH, LOVE MANAGING A LIVE GAME!

Karen K. Lee

WHAT'S A LIVE GAME?

In the earlier days of gaming, single-release games were the main types of games you'd see. Studios worked hard to complete a game, which was then released for sale to the world – and that was that. If the title saw great success, we'd usually see a sequel or a branch off of the game such as in the case of *Super Mario Bros* and *Super Mario Bros 2*, and now we get all sorts of fun stuff like *Super Mario Party* and *Mario Kart*!

As gaming transformed, a new type of game catered to the want from both the community and developers to continually build on a persisting game experience. This led us to what we call live service games (or simply: live games). With continual updates, fixes, and new content, live games have become incredibly popular. Some of them are home to the largest player counts in the world. You've likely been a part of one live game or another, whether it's a classic like the MMORPG *World of Warcraft*, or the more recent rounds of *Among Us* you may have played with your friends. While consoles and PCs explored the live game territory earlier on, mobile games have proven to thrive off the world of live service, and we're seeing the quality of mobile games go exponentially up.

Before I keep moving forward, I should introduce myself. I'm Karen K. Lee and have had years of experience being a game community developer. Most of my experience lies with live games. I started off in game community management on a mobile title, and then also worked on projects that spanned various platforms including *Rainbow Six Siege* and *Apex Legends*. I'm passionate about continuing to develop lasting spaces where game communities can grow alongside a game that is ever-evolving. I find that the world of live games is exciting as there is always new content and unique challenges to face.

A well-run live game can last for many years, bringing entertainment and a sense of belonging to both the development team and the community that surrounds it. If you're soon to embark on a quest to manage a live game community, there are key nuances you should keep in mind to help you and the community you manage succeed.

PARTNERS

While your main role is to be in touch with the community, an important part of live game community management is being in tune with your game's development team. Since the game you work on is constantly in flux, being on top of what direction it's going in and what changes will come will enable you to better prepare communications or initiatives shaped around them. As you get a real sense of the community you're working with and learn their patterns of reception to releases, you can also help lend insight into how players might perceive upcoming content.

Something that I've found to be helpful on most of the live games I've worked on is to keep an open channel with your live operations team. The live operations team knows when and what will go out with coming updates. You will want to speak to them so you've got a full list of bug fixes and any other known issues they might preemptively be able to flag. There might also be times when certain features have to get turned on or off, which is important to convey to your players. On the flip side, it's also important to flag major issues you're seeing to the live operations team so they can see what can be prioritised in a hotfix or upcoming patch.

Outside of the folks building the game, you'll also have to work in tandem with your brand, marketing, and communication partners. With every new season or content update, these are likely the colleagues you'll have to sync up with to figure out when and how major announcements will go out to the community and beyond.

Regardless of how big the overall team working on your live game is, it's a good habit to set up expectations and recurring routines that your partner can rely on you for. That includes when patch notes are expected to go live with updates or how many lead days you might need to produce a dev blog with development teams. On the other hand, learning the customary release window for when new trailers might drop or when press releases get sent out can help you better plan your initiatives' release windows too. This helps not only your internal partners, but also helps set up a cadence with the community you interface with. Which brings us to…

THE COMMUNITY

The community is why we're all here, right?! You've heard lots about the importance and value that game communities can bring to your game, but what about live games in particular?

In live games, there are endless pieces of content going out with every update. This is where things can get fun on a live title: find ways to fold your community into the game you're working on! Whether it's in feedback sessions or involving community artists to contribute cosmetics to your game, there's a lot of runway for you to engage and involve community members. If there's a lack of bandwidth on the game team side for integrating community-created art into the upcoming season, there might be a chance down the road. The coming update won't have an early enough playtest build that you can get in front of a community focus group? See if you can work with the game team to try to execute on a playtest next season!

Another key part of running communities in a live game is to seek out and uplift your community leaders. Your game will continue to evolve over every update. Knowing who your advocates are and helping them grow their communities alongside the game will help both parties in the long run. Retention of your community leaders and consequently the general player base helps to keep your game healthy. After all, your game can only continue to run if there are players who continue to enjoy the game. Identify, empower, and involve your community leaders!

LAST TIPS

There's a lot more to the world of live games and I can go on forever. But I would like to leave two last tips here for those looking into, or getting started in, live games. First, get a cycle going with your game's updates so that you and your team don't feel overwhelmed by the continuous content. You don't have to reinvent every part of the wheel every time. There are elements that your partners and the community will learn to depend on and expect as the game goes through different seasons. That said, also learn how to deviate from bits of the cycle so that you have space to try out new things – and also keep the community and dev team engaged. Look out for holidays, causes, community leaders, and community events that you might be able to lean into on top of the scheduled game releases. There's a lot of inspiration both in and out of the game to keep things fresh!

My last, and likely most important, tip for those in live games is this: it's a marathon, not a sprint. Don't race to the finish line because a healthy live game won't have one for a good while. Burning out can be a terrifying experience and if you're not taking care of yourself, you can't take care of the community of players and developers that you work with. Pace yourself, work out a cadence, and keep getting inspired as your game develops. I wish you the best of luck in the world of live games!

7.2 CREATING SHARED EXPERIENCES

Communities, by definition, require people to come together, united by a shared motivation or passion. As a CM, you should strive to encourage social interaction among your players, regardless of whether they play a multi- or single-player game. Gaming has helped create real-life, long-lasting friendships for decades[1]. The COVID-19 pandemic has cemented the role games can play in bringing people together and reducing feelings of loneliness. We can actively support this. It's one of the things I love most about my job. Ask yourself: *how can I help people connect to other humans*? Identify what options the game gives players and what sets it apart from others. If you're working on a multiplayer game, you could experiment with challenges rewarding players who collaborate best with others or help newcomers. For single-player games, encourage those who create guides or create in-game content. You could go further and implement titles on your forums or Discord for players actively seeking to support those with questions. Think about it as an onboarding ramp for your community where more experienced members band together with newer ones, hoping to turn them into seasoned veterans. The possibilities for community initiatives are limitless and depend mostly on your imagination (and your community budget). I've heard of CMs organising weekly gaming tournaments, both online and offline. My community has been doing quiz nights and game sessions open to everyone over Discord voice chat. Of course, we communicate basic ground rules, and there's always a moderator present who participates in conversations and makes sure everything stays friendly. Similarly, support community members if they want to meet up and organise unofficial community gatherings – or go ahead and create official meetups if you can! Explicitly show the value of being an active part of the community. This value can be anything. During one particularly grey November, we told our community we'd be happy to send holiday greetings to anyone needing some kind words. While writing personalised notes for dozens of people took a lot of time, it was worth the effort. Everyone got themed cookies as a surprise gift, and the reception was incredible. Another thing we organised was a small token for the active founding members of our German-speaking section of one Discord channel. Because we'd been theming a lot of our campaign around music, we produced custom festival wristbands with the game's logo and the relevant hashtag for our community. It required almost no budget, and it created a bonding element for everyone who initially supported us.

One common topic when talking to CMs is *lurkers*. You might've also heard the term mentioned by streamers about people not participating in chats. It's somewhat derogatory, as if people are maliciously taking things from the community without giving back. As a notorious lurker in numerous communities myself, that's usually not true. Often, people don't actively participate because they feel they have nothing valuable to contribute. Your job will largely revolve around those people and your shared journey to encourage them to let others partake in their opinions, knowledge, or creations. Make it explicit and regularly repeat that everyone's contribution counts. You'll have to constantly improve your information pipeline to assist inactive community members because they're not yet engaged enough to stick around when frustrated.

I cannot tell you which experiences will bring your community members closer together. No two groups of people are the same, after all. There's only one solution: get to know them, find out what they've been missing from your company or others, observe conversations when they don't even realise you're reading, and then experiment and iterate. It's worth it.

7.3 PUTTING THE SPOTLIGHT ON COMMUNITY AND DEVS

It bears repeating that CMs are among the most publicly visible members of a game studio if they choose to put their names to the job. They help players forge a human connection with the studio. I know *humanising a company* may sound like a buzzword, but don't dismiss it immediately. There'll always be people who accuse companies of being insincere. Still, if done well, your projects show players the breathing, living people behind the brand.

Community streams are great examples of this. Responding to your community's questions, walking them through game updates, or taking time to react to their feedback will spread knowledge and create advocates who then disperse into subgroups of your community to share it further. If conversations revolve around technical aspects of your game, bring someone from the development team onboard to enrich the talk. If you don't want to appear on-screen yourself, equip another spokesperson with the required community knowledge and act as a producer. Are you dropping an update with a change to the game's rendering? Let someone who worked on it share their expertise. Is your game being localised to a new language? Highlight the voice actors and the recording team to show their work behind the scenes. People make games; remind everyone from time to time.

Similarly, remember that community work means interacting with humans, not just numbers and on-screen avatars. Engaging with a game you love on a creative level is a deeply personal matter. If you didn't care about something, you wouldn't draw fan art, invest lots of time and money into cosplay, write guides, or film video tutorials. CMs should never take this engagement for granted. Actively seek these creations out. Even dropping a like or an appreciative comment can make someone's day. Create highlight reels, share fan creations on your social channels (tag the original creator!), or interview them for your forums. Treat them with respect, and I guarantee it won't go unnoticed.

7.4 A SHORT TANGENT ON PROJECT MANAGEMENT

One crucial aspect that has helped me is my background in project management. Familiarising yourself with planning, tracking progress and timelines, and setting goals will be invaluable in your career since your job is made up of huge (release campaigns), medium (setting up a code of conduct), and smaller (sale announcement) projects. While they differ in complexity, the pillars of approaching them are the same. I won't go too deep into project management here, but I highly recommend you read some in-depth books on the topic.[2] However, some things can save you a lot of stress and time, so consider them from the beginning.

7.4.1 Setting Goals

Many people need to hear this: *creating something viral* isn't a great goal. What is *virality*, and how do you know if you've achieved it, anyway? Similarly, please don't copy a list of *great goals for your indie game campaign*. Your goals should be strongly intertwined with your strategy, and both should inform each other. In the best-case scenario, your company has overall goals for the game from which you derive a strategy and set your goals to ensure you reach what you're setting out to do. Don't set goals within a vacuum. Unless you're the only person in your company working outside of hands-on game development, you'll find existing communication and marketing goals to align yours with. An established theory refers to effective goals as SMART. Following it has helped me improve my work over the last few years. So, what does it mean? Every goal you set should ideally be specific, measurable, achievable, relevant, and timely.

Specific is basically your goal's elevator pitch. In a concise statement, answer what you want to accomplish, why, with whom, where, and which barriers you might face or resources you can draw on. In my example of *making something go viral*, adding specificity might include what engagement numbers (incl. impressions) you're looking for, which channel you want to focus on, who the most important community influencers are, and which other aspects of your strategy this builds on for saving resources. Specificity adds value to your goal and immediately helps form a clearer picture of what you should tackle.

There are numerous ways you can *measure* success. You might feel the urge to fight back against the notion that everything has to be measurable. What a cold way of looking at interpersonal relationships, right? Am I telling you to reduce all your projects to numbers and click-through rates? If my tone isn't giving it away: this isn't what this means. When setting a goal, ask yourself how you'll know you've achieved it. If someone asks you to create a viral post, ask, "What are your criteria for virality?" Your goals should allow you to track progress towards them and give you a tangible feeling of being *done* instead of constantly wondering if you've done enough. You could measure the percentage of engaged users, the number of submissions to a contest, sign-ups for an event, or the sentiment after an update.

The *achievable* dimension of setting a great goal has two aspects. First: is the overall goal achievable if you consider financial, personnel, and other constraints? Second: do you have any influence over the goal?

Ideally, your goals should ask you to strive for something beyond your immediate reach. But for example, if you're asked to create a content creator outreach programme that will lead your game into the Top 10 most streamed games over a given timeframe, you won't be able to do this with $1000. If you do, you're a wizard. Take a realistic inventory of what you have at your disposal and what kind of goal you can achieve. If your boss asks you to achieve the goal above, respond with a counterproposal. Perhaps you could focus on collaborating with smaller streamers to get your game covered by genre enthusiasts instead of targeting only mainstream ones.

The second aspect isn't 100% necessary for a good goal but keep it in mind for setting a *great* one. Of course, you can set a goal that isn't within your control and do certain things that don't directly feed into it, but still achieve it. Setting yourself the goal of achieving *Overwhelmingly Positive* user scores on Steam isn't within your control unless you're also coding, bug-fixing, and designing the game. What you can work towards are goals such as *Respond to x per cent of Steam Reviews,* or *Forward x per cent of community reports to the development team.* That being said, you can contribute towards the wider company goal of achieving that Overwhelmingly Positive sentiment as long as it's a shared effort across departments.

As luck would have it, that example leads perfectly to the explanation of *relevant*: Does your goal fit the wider vision of your department or company? Ideally, your company has a vision broken down into successively smaller goals, from grand-scale marketing goals to one set within the communications department, informing yours as a CM. We only have limited time, so we have to prioritise. Maybe it's also not the right time for other goals; you're convinced that something really has to be done, you have a framework in mind of how you could achieve it, but it doesn't fit what the company wants right now. It happens. Make a note in your trusted self-management tool and keep it for later.[3]

For your goal to be *timely*, you need to have a deadline. If you weren't given a deadline, make one up. Break it down into the smaller steps you need to take to achieve your goal. Assign required hours to each step to create milestones in your timeline. Apart from the happiness boost of checking things off your to-do list, it keeps you on track for the bigger goal. Say you're planning to write a book. *Writing 40,000 words* sounds insurmountable and paralysing. Writing *400 words a day* or *2,800 words a week* is concrete, manageable, and – if you follow it – will bring you to the goal you once thought impossible.

Usually, it's wisest to calculate backwards to set appropriate deadlines. When do you want to reach your goal? Do you need to factor in approval time? Does your goal require the work of another department? Does someone's work depend on that department? In any game company, there are basically unlimited variations of dependencies, and reasonable project management should allow for feedback, approvals, holidays, and sickness. As a rule of thumb, if I think something takes one month, I give it two. Is it excessive? Maybe. But life happens, and if you have the luxury of setting deadlines for your goals, you should be realistic. If you're met with deadlines that seem unreasonable and cannot be moved in any way, dissect the goal to see what you need to achieve until when. Maybe two elements can happen parallel to reduce idle time, or approval can be sped up by bundling it with something else.

There have been many valuable discussions about the value of SMART goals and whether they're still valid since the theory's inception in 1981. But you don't have to concern yourself with these in the early stages of your career. Once you have a solid grasp on your job and are interested in learning more, you can dive deeper. Until then, remember not to charge ahead alone and don't hyperfocus on a single, siloed goal. This industry thrives on collaboration, and the same applies to your goals. Align with your team, ask them for their insight, and keep a flexible mindset. If your situation changes, don't force yourself to stick to goals you've set in a different context – adapt them. It's easier to tweak them as you go along when you have smaller goals that feed into your few, bigger ones, and it's also less painful to fail to achieve some goals when you have several more that you've successfully reached.

7.4.2 Preparing Budgets

Every company works differently. Instead of having to create budget proposals, you might get handed a fixed budget and have to figure out what to do with it. Or maybe you'll get no budget at all, in which case I'm rooting for you to get some wiggle room in the future. Even when there's little budget to work with, you should understand how much different community activities can cost, how to prioritise your needs, and what to spend money on. If there's something you've always thought would be the best project ever, and you're astonished that seemingly no one's had this idea yet … chances are it probably died in someone's budget meeting. Regardless of how high the community budget is, try to diversify your activities and don't fall prey to the temptation of spending it all on one thing. You want to keep people engaged for longer than a single window of time.

Sometimes people wonder why CMs require any budget in the first place. Granted, many things in our jobs can indeed be done for free and it helps to train to be as scrappy as possible. But if you want to organise an event, commission artists, work with content creators, run contests, have small gifts for community members visiting the office, or have moderators, we're quickly talking about a lot of money. Hopefully you can advocate for your community's financial needs, lay out why your budget requests make sense for the company, and then make sure that whatever money you have is well-spent.

If you get to request a budget, do your research. List everything you might need and write average costs down next to individual elements. Be realistic and consider buffer costs of at least 10%. Next, categorise and prioritise all elements. What can't you work without, and what qualifies as a cherry on top? This helps prevent over- or underbudgeting certain areas. Make sure to cover the basics, too. Depending on the company, some things might fall into other teams' responsibilities, but it never hurts to double-check.

Some things you could think about including:

*   Moderator payment (if you have a budget, pay the humans helping you)
*   Shipping (goodies, greeting cards …)
*   Merchandise purchases (for contests, creator gifts …)
*   Commissions (illustrations, cosplays …)
*   Event travel
*   Community events (venue, catering, photographer …)
*   Seeding (getting your game into the hands of community ambassadors)
*   Agency costs (websites, creative …)

With budgets, remember to always consider the why, not only the what. How does this money feed into your goals and the wider company strategy? You should have a compelling answer if you're asked why you want to spend the company's money.

7.4.3 Keeping Track of Your Things

What method works best to track your projects depends greatly on your preferences. If you're not managing other people, you can pick whatever works best for you. Your company may require you to update project statuses in specific tools, which you should obviously do – but updating project statuses isn't the same as keeping track of your own work. There are numerous free or paid tools you can try. Be it a Kanban board, a project tracker, or a physical notebook. Whatever you land on, be consistent.

Did you promise a team member to forward an email? Have you sent out a request? Write it down and follow up. Do you work on a complex activation with so many tasks you don't know where to start? Break it down into the smallest units, turn them into a checklist, and then work on the steps individually. When you write down anything, be precise and give clear titles so you know what it's about at one glance. Provide enough context to remember what it means a week later. "Finish report by tomorrow" may sound good when you write it down, but if you go back to the note a couple of days later, you may wonder which report you were referring to and what date *tomorrow* was supposed to be. If you already have valuable resources and you're keeping track of your things digitally, link to all these documents wherever you keep the update.

You may ask yourself why you should be this meticulous. Firstly, we're always sure we'll remember something significant until three different things come up, and that thing has wholly left our brains. Secondly, tracking your progress, promises, and tasks ensures you're moving towards your goals and – if you're anything like me – will help calm that inner voice that tells you you're not doing any work. Last, following up on promises and being responsive makes you a better and more reliable colleague.

7.5 BEING A FORCE FOR GOOD

Your CM style is very personal and there's no one right way to do the job. Instead, you'll go through the toolbox to pick and choose what suits you and develop your own style.

> There isn't one way of being a good community manager. You can admire one, but just because you don't work the same way or aren't as popular doesn't mean you're not good. Remember your community management type depends on many things, so it will be different from a company and community to another.
>
> —— MARION MY ANH
>   BAXERRES

If there's one thing you internalise about the role, I hope it's this: I don't believe it's enough to not be a negative influence. We have the power to design spaces and experiences that positively impact people. Not working towards an inclusive, enriching community seems like a wasted opportunity. There are also benefits for the company. Simply said, a company's community becomes part of its brand image. They'll speak for you in corners of the Internet outside of your control. They might sport avatars connected to your brand while posting hateful messages or engage in behaviour that is generally unacceptable. Some people might never read any of your communication but have an image in their minds because of how your audience conducts itself. They speak for you, whether you encourage it or not. The more your game relies on social interaction between people, the more a community with a bad reputation can cost you players that want to avoid harmful experiences. Of course, you won't be able to influence the online behaviour of everyone in your community, but you can set the tone for what's acceptable. So, the million-dollar question is – how do you create a positive community?

7.5.1 Modelling Behaviour

The first step is straightforward; model the behaviour you want to see. If you want people to be kind and helpful, you shouldn't behave in a snarky and dismissive manner all day. It should go without saying that acts that would get your community members blocked or suspended are entirely off the table for you. That doesn't mean you have to be all hearts and rainbows, and abstain from jokes or tough decisions, but it does mean behaving like a role model for your ideal community. Do you want to see your community show compassion when others are stressed? A message showing that you remember someone's milestone or asking about their day if they seem off can go a long way. Similarly, understand the role you're playing now. You're a representative of the company. For better or worse, this makes you at least a curiosity to speak to. I had to get used to this initially because some people will go to great lengths to get you to react to them. Trolling and hateful messages are often meant to elicit any response – since that's still better than being ignored. But what happens if people see you respond mainly to negative messages and not reward positivity? You might end up incentivising toxic behaviour. Many years ago, I listened to a presentation where someone said, "If you're tending to your garden, you focus on watering the flowers, not the weed." So that's my main message for you: water your flowers. Thank people for leaving nice comments. Go out of your way to acknowledge people helping others with guides or linking to news articles. Shine a light on community creations if you're lucky enough to have such an engaged community. You could even go so far as to provide a surprise reward if the community is on an overall streak of positivity. This isn't to say you should ignore valid criticism and feedback. On the contrary, you should react to it with gratitude and attention. From where I'm standing, that's highly positive behaviour – if we understand positivity as an action that works towards improving the space and experience for everyone. If someone cares enough to provide actionable feedback instead of just being negative or abandoning the game altogether, keep that person around.

7.5.2 Code of Conduct

I've talked about negative and positive behaviour and about acting the way you want others to behave, so you might wonder how to decide what's okay and what isn't. I'm sure you've developed a trusted gut feeling; however, a community shouldn't be run solely based on that, even if it's right. The rules of acceptable behaviour, often called the *code of conduct*, should be available in writing and visible in multiple places. For example, you could create pinned posts on your forums and Discord, have them as PDFs on your website, and link to them on other social media platforms. Be transparent with your community about what to expect from you and others. Having these guidelines also holds you accountable and prevents drastic changes in moderation if you onboard additional assistance. It also protects you from looking arbitrary if you need to ban people. You posted your house rules, people broke them, they got banned. Simple. A code of conduct makes it harder to turn this into discussions about personal feelings or biases.

Now, what should a code of conduct look like? You shouldn't reinvent the wheel in case your company already has one, as it should be one unified code of conduct across all games, platforms, and regions. Treat the code of conduct as one of the most important documents for your job and familiarise yourself with it intimately. Once you start interacting with your community regularly, you must be the living embodiment of this document. Should something in the rules confuse you or feel outdated, please don't hesitate to contact your boss and explain why you think it's time to update the document.

You've asked your colleagues, and scoured internal resources, but you cannot find a code of conduct. This is pretty exciting for you because it's time to create one! Arm yourself with arguments about why this document should exist and offer to handle the process. Make sure to involve other departments if necessary; depending on the size of your company's operations, it might be that the legal department or the localisation team have to assist you. Again, exciting! That's a great project that allows you to work with others and have something tangible and impactful as the result. Once your lead approves you to move forward, start laying out what you deem most important for your community. Refer to other company materials, such as the mission statement, so everything's unified.

Now begins the time to make decisions – what do you want to include in the code, and what do you consider unacceptable behaviour? Start with bullet points and work from there. Most aspects you want to list should be self-explanatory. For example, everyone wishing to participate in your in-person events, create community content, or participate in your community in any other way commits to honouring your house rules; no harassment of any kind and on any basis is permitted; no harmful behaviour will be accepted, including sharing pictures, videos, or text messages that either negatively impact a community member directly or make them feel unsafe in your space. Be as specific as possible, so people cannot argue that you were too vague. In my case, I also don't accept extremely disparaging conversations about other game developers or their creations. Of course, discussing and criticising companies and games is completely fine – you want people to feel like they can discuss their passions – but my line is drawn where things turn disrespectful. Furthermore, make it crystal clear what kind of behaviour warrants a warning, and what constitutes a suspension or ban. People must have a clear, transparent, and understandable overview of actions and consequences.

Another thing to include in the code of conduct is a way to report a violation if you're not there to witness it. No matter how small the community, you won't be able to see everything. Thus, your community needs a straightforward way to inform you if someone has violated the rules. Once you've announced the code to your community, enforce it. Don't let reported violations slide without investigating them and taking action. If you're working in a group, talk to all other community and social media managers and moderators about the rules of escalation. When people get banned, remind them and the community that this is due to violating the code of conduct. Otherwise, your community might treat it as mere lip service and ignore it.

7.5.3 Find Allies in Your Community

Sadly, toxicity often shapes our conversations on- and offline about gaming communities. That's why it's crucial to find people who are continuously supportive of your game, interact with your content, and help you spread positivity. While these traits can be found in many community members, I want to focus on a subset that is very dear to my heart and without whom CMs would all erupt into flames: moderators.

Treat them well, and they'll make your experience much more efficient and pleasurable. Looking at everything you do in your workday, you'll quickly realise that you cannot always be active in all your community spaces. Even if you spend eight hours there daily, remember that time zones exist. It's unlikely that everyone in your community lives in the same region. Thus, when you stop working, someone from your community will wake up or return home from work or school to engage with others. Carefully selected moderators help mitigate this issue. Recruit from within your community as much as possible – they know about your games and the people making your community unique. If your moderators speak an additional language or cover another region, they can also reach out to new people. Keep track of those who are active and kind in your community, help others, and keep a level head in discussions. Those are the people you want to support. On the other hand, someone who's always just wanted to be able to ban people or dictate how others can talk about games should never be put into an important position like this. If they are, toxicity and unhappiness will soon run rampant.

If you have no pre-existing community to recruit from, do some friendly espionage. Scout in communities with a similar focus to find the right people. Introduce yourself and your company, and get straight to the point. Tell them why you reached out and ask whether they'd be interested in working with you. In both cases, vet them. Check their social media channels or previous chat behaviour because you'll want to avoid any nasty surprises down the line. If you hire someone who has said terrible things in the past, it'll reflect on your company if people find out. At least do a Google search of their (user) name. If no red flags appear, see if they have spare time to take on moderation duties and earn money. This is your reminder to pay moderators. Don't exploit their passion. The only exception I'll allow is smaller indie studios that don't have the resources yet. In that case, lay this out transparently to align expectations early. But if your company is mid-sized or above? No excuses.

Once you have your first moderator on board, treat them like royalty. Make their work experience as comfortable as possible, and provide guidelines about moderation style, your code of conduct, and appropriate wordings. What can they decide by themselves, and what kind of cases should they consult you on? These rules will become crucial once you have more than one moderator, as you'll want to avoid scenarios where moderators can be pitted against one another or get a reputation for being *harsh* or *soft*.

Your moderators will enforce any rules you lay out, identify issues before they escalate, find potential community ambassadors or additional moderators, and improve the quality of your space. Ensure they can easily contact you if they need your help. If they provide feedback, listen. They're incredibly close to the community, and people often tell them things they might not feel comfortable telling you directly. This is especially true if you work for a bigger studio where community members sometimes hesitate to *bother* the

CM. Even if you try addressing this mindset to encourage more direct communication, having someone work alongside you for people to approach with feedback is invaluable. In turn, protect your moderators. Don't challenge their authority in public. If they ban someone, and that person complains to you, don't tell them the moderator made a wrong decision. This undercuts any future decisions they make and erodes their trust in you. Instead, reach out to them in private. Mention something wasn't done according to the rules or share people's complaints so they're aware of them – and of the fact that you trust them enough to tell them.

It shouldn't have to be said, but if you see someone insulting or harassing your moderators, step in. Depending on the severity, warn or block the offender outright. If you see your moderators struggle, check what you can do for them. My colleagues and I also give moderators access to events reserved for press, send them merchandise, and make sure they know we appreciate them. And they should receive free game keys as a minimum. Establishing a great relationship with your moderators is one of the most crucial aspects of your success. Trust me.

That covers the various aspects of how to get moderators, but what about the when? There's no simple answer, as it also depends on the type of game. Is your game competitive or a cosy experience? What's the average age of your target audience? On average, the younger and more competitive, the more moderation I'd plan for. As I've mentioned, if your game is popular in another time zone, onboard a moderator from that region as quickly as possible to cover your off time, even if you think your game is technically small enough to cover alone. If your existing moderators tell you they're overburdened with work, or you get multiple messages from community members that their feedback isn't acknowledged appropriately, it might be time to hire another person. The absolute latest time to bring in a moderator: the moment your community grows to a size where you cannot do it justice while still doing your regular work.

7.5.4 Trolls and the Beauty of the Ban-Hammer

Let's balance it out and talk about the other side of the positivity coin. Negative online actions can broadly be grouped into two categories: trolling and hate speech. As hard as it is, try not to take harsh behaviour personally. If you've spent any time online, you know trolls are just an unavoidable part of the package. I don't believe this is a distinctly modern phenomenon – tricksters, ignorant, or rude people have always existed – but today's level of connectedness is unprecedented. Increasingly, our social interactions happen in digital spaces. Why am I telling you this? Because I don't want you to blame yourself if you do your best and trolls still frequent your community.

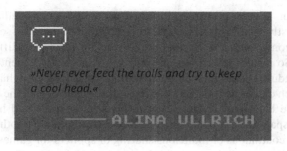

»Never ever feed the trolls and try to keep a cool head.«

—— ALINA ULLRICH

You know what trolls are. You most likely face them daily. Frankly speaking, you've probably been one yourself, occasionally. The line between humour and abuse can be blurry. In-jokes and accepted language vary greatly across cultures and demographics. Countless discussions exist about what constitutes trolling and why people engage in abusive behaviour. For our purpose, though, it isn't crucial to have an airtight definition. What matters is that you know what it looks like. If I had to paraphrase it, I'd say trolling is purposeful behaviour to disrupt online conversations or provoke emotional reactions. This doesn't always include insults and verbal violence. For the most part, trolls know precisely what they're doing and want to prevent being excluded from a community.

Hate speech is a whole other beast. Telling someone they should end their lives or threatening physical abuse doesn't exist on a scale of grey. As the name says, this behaviour is defined by hateful and violent messages, often connected with discrimination based on aspects such as race, gender, religion, or disability. In recent years, we've also seen a rise in hate speech rooted in different political beliefs with the potential of inciting offline violence. This isn't the place to explain why humans engage in this behaviour, the role bots play, or why our societies feel more fractured. I couldn't do the topic justice in the context of this book. But if you're working with online communities in any capacity, please read up on this.[4]

Trolling has several reasons: people are bored, enjoy the attention, are hurt and lash out or want to ruin other people's enjoyment. Those things are outside of your control. What isn't is how you react to them. You've probably heard of the credo, "Don't feed the trolls." While it can be satisfying to dunk on trolls, when handling brand accounts, I strongly advise against it – unless the whole company has decided to make edginess its brand identity. But remember, trolls generally behave this way to get attention. Outrage or public scolding still gives them that. If you want to have fewer trolls, don't give them a megaphone to amplify their voice. Depending on the severity of the action and the platform, you have several options: ignore, mute/shadow-ban, or block/ban. I won't go through all options on all social media platforms because, firstly, platforms change features regularly, and this section could quickly become outdated. Secondly, the relevant platforms differ between countries. So instead, I'll focus on what you can do. As I mentioned, your code of conduct should include details about what kind of behaviour earns people which consequences. Be open about the effects of specific behaviours. Sanctionable behaviour includes any form of harassment and hate speech, purposeful spamming or spreading of leaks, self-promotion of other games or creators, or continuous or malicious sharing of spoilers for games.

It's your responsibility to keep the community healthy. To achieve this, you not only have to reward positive community members but also get rid of toxic ones. Don't feel bad for doing this. You communicated the rules clearly and they chose to break them. Actions have consequences. Furthermore, I want to shift your perspective. The ban-hammer is your weapon to defend other community members. You're wielding it to make others feel more comfortable expressing themselves. There's a myth you cannot ban a toxic person if they're an active community member. I've read about the fear of creating silence and killing engagement. However, this toxic person might have participated a lot, but their behaviour kept many others from engaging. Be fair, be transparent, and be consistent. And then ban everyone who deserves it according to your rules – without guilt.

I need to point out again: criticism and negative feedback are valuable. Unless it's phrased violently, don't ban or mute people for being negative about your company. Providing proper feedback is a positive act. It means that people care. Punishing people for that makes your company look arrogant, dismissive, or worse. But here's the beauty: creating a safe community where toxic people get sanctioned might encourage even more players to share positive and negative feedback, enabling you to be more successful at helping your company improve.

7.6 ACCESSIBILITY IN COMMUNITY MANAGEMENT
Paige Harvey

When people talk about accessibility in games, it's often discussed in terms of access to a game itself, whether that's through options for improved motor accessibility, consideration for colour-blindness, or myriad other options to tweak a game to the player's level of comfort and ease.

However, there's an area of accessibility not often discussed when it comes to making video games, and that's in marketing and community management.

Games communities are wonderfully diverse, intersectional, and full of people both alike and unlike you – and it's our job as CMs to try and account for the needs of as many community members as possible. I'll explain some of the methods in which you can tailor your communications and improve your current accessibility offerings.

SOCIAL MEDIA, FORUMS, AND DISCORD

When marketing a game or managing a community, you'll often use a variety of social media platforms to engage and inform, whether that's through text or visual assets. When writing a social post, consider the following:

- **Is the text you've written easy to understand and to physically read?** Some users may use a screen reader, some may use translators to read in a language they are more comfortable with. Consider your choice of words and how those words are written for example, "Wow!," is easier to understand than "Wooooooooow!"
- **What extras have you added to your text?** Try to limit the amount of emojis used in a single post, as screen readers will read the name of each out individually.
- **How is your text presented?** Avoid using fancy fonts and symbols as these could cause issues for screen readers, neurodivergent people, and others.
- **How easy are your hashtags to understand?** When using a string of words in a hashtag, be sure to use "Camel Casing," and start each word with a capital letter. This ensures readability, and that screen readers will read the hashtag correctly.
- **Have you included an image, GIF, or video?** Be sure to provide alt text, a short description of the visual asset used to provide context to people using screen readers and should be concise and informative. Don't use alt text to share jokes, hide information, or poke fun.

When you're satisfied with the copy you've written, always try to seek a second opinion who can check your writing is comprehensible, spelled correctly, and easy to understand.

EMAILS AND MESSAGES

As a CM, you'll spend a lot of time speaking with others via email and direct messages, often without really knowing the person on the other end. To facilitate easy communication, try to consider the following points alongside the points listed in the previous section "Social Media, Forums, and Discord":

- **Do you need to receive an answer via text?** Some people may find it easier to communicate via text – while a recording or call might be easier for others – so try to offer multiple communication options.
- **How are your communications presented?** Keep the format of your emails and messages easily readable by using a unified layout, standard font, and simple colour palette. Consider that your emails may not be received in plain text, so don't rely on imagery and embedded elements.

VISUAL ASSETS

Throughout the promotion and ongoing management of any game, you'll likely release images and videos on social and video-sharing platforms. Though each platform has its own rules and accessibility options available, there are some things that you can control to help your content be seen by as many people as possible. When crafting or posting a visual asset, consider the following:

- **Does your asset contain text?** Try to ensure your text is in an easy-to-read font, that the colour contrasts comfortably against the background and that, where applicable, you've added an outline to help define each character.
- **How is your asset laid out and presented?** Try to keep each element distinct and complimentary by not adding too many details into a single image. Consider using a tool to visualise how your asset may look for members of your community with colour-blindness.
- **Does your asset contain triggering material?** For anything that could trigger physical or mental distress, a content warning should be given. For example, you could provide a warning for sudden loud sounds, flashing lights, fast or shaky movement, disturbing content or traumatic discussion points.
- **Does your asset have audio that needs to be understood?** Providing access to your video assets through captioning, closed-captioning, or videoed sign language is a great way

to include your audience and can be of great help for deaf people, those with auditory processing conditions, and those whose safety relies on keeping a device silent.

LIVESTREAMING

You may be responsible for managing and/or running livestreams for your company. The accessibility measures you may want to utilise for livestreams are similar to those we've already discussed; however, they are presented differently in a live situation. Try to consider the following:

- **How do you introduce yourself?** Consider describing yourself and inviting stream guests to do the same when you start a stream. For example, you could give your name, a short description of your appearance, and your pronouns.
- **How will you provide for community members who can't hear?** Depending on your budget, you may consider adding one of the following accessibility measures; you can use a free captioning system or hire a live captioning service to add a text-to-speech feed to your stream, and you could also consider hiring someone fluent in sign language to live-translate your stream.
- **Does your stream contain triggering material?** Like visual assets, your streams may contain triggering content, especially if you're streaming gameplay. Consider adding any trigger warnings to your stream's title – or having an emergency "Content Warning" screen to cover any visuals on your screen while you manage the stream.
- **Is your stream branding appropriate?** Avoid utilising flashing or jump-scare alerts for notifications – and consider looking through in the previous section "Visual Assets" when designing overlays for your stream!

7.7 WHAT TO DO WHEN THINGS GO WRONG

No matter how well you prepare yourself, sometimes you'll mess up. To err is human. Maybe you didn't double-check your messaging before publishing it. Maybe community members managed to rile you up enough for you to lash out. Especially at the beginning of your career, making mistakes isn't only normal but also necessary for growth, but the lesson does hit home differently when you have to explain to your boss or your community what you did wrong and why. Making a mistake won't define how people see you, but it's how you deal with it that people will remember. My most important advice: accountability. You messed up. Don't try to deny it or point fingers. Think through the mistake and why you made it. Be analytical and as rational as possible. If other people contributed to you making a mistake, make a note, but don't play the blame game. If you made an error only visible within your company, talk to the affected people and apologize, if necessary. Sit down with your lead, lay out concisely what you could've done better, and explain how you plan to avoid similar mistakes in the future. Any publicly visible mistakes shouldn't be swept under the rug. I understand the impulse of burying your head in the sand and waiting for the situation to pass. Some years ago, I ran a local contest. Then I fell sick shortly before the contest ended. Instead of actively working towards a solution by finding someone to substitute for me, I figured I'd surely be healthy again in time … and then I was too sick to even think about it. In hindsight, my mistake is clear. I should've asked for help when I saw the chance I couldn't deliver on my promise to the community. After briefly screaming into my pillow, I published a message acknowledging my mistake and addressing that it happened due to a health problem. Was it the right approach for everyone? Probably not. But you should find a way to openly own up to your mistakes. In the long run, that'll increase the trust level between you and your community.

Community Management can be heaven or hell for those who do the job. [...] Stay cool, listen to people and when they have the feeling that they are heard and that you understand them and talk to them, they will be thankful and forgiving.

———— BENJAMIN

So far, I've talked about you having to own up to a mistake you made. But there's also another option which is much more complex – the company making a mistake and you being part of the team that needs to devise a solution. It's doubtful you'll face this issue alone, but it can be extremely overwhelming regardless. Just trust me on this. Observe as much as possible. Crisis communication is a valuable skill that will help you tremendously in your future career in communications. Problems worthy of crisis communication can range from smaller hiccups, such as a patch that didn't land well, to company scandals revealed by whistle-blowers. You'll be included if your help is required, but what can you do proactively or if no one can guide you? Evaluate, de-escalate, solve.

First, evaluate the situation. The success of all upcoming steps hinges on your understanding of what went wrong and why. If people are directly affected, figure out how many and at which levels. Is everyone experiencing the same issue, or are certain people more affected than others? Are many people experiencing the issue themselves or are they amplifying the issue of others, thus making it look bigger? Even trickier: are the ones talking about it members of your community, people with multiple accounts, or bots? What you're trying to figure out is whether you're facing a major public issue or a vocal minority. Should there be several layers to the problem, track them individually. When a situation is particularly heated, you might be tempted to immediately issue a public statement. That's fine if we're talking about simple misunderstandings you can correct with a brief update. But if the issue is more complex, you can make the situation worse by prematurely talking about it.

Make no early promises. Your first goal is to understand every aspect of the problem. That'll be important later because you might require different de-escalation and solution strategies. Take notes of everything connected to the problem; once you believe you have a complete picture, it's time to move on. Share the results of your research with your colleagues. See if you can actively contribute to the next steps. If that's not possible, don't take it personally. There might be a tried-and-tested process in the company already in place. If you're able to work with the team or oversee addressing the issue, it's time for the next step.

Don't devalue criticism but work towards de-escalation and providing necessary information. Action speaks louder than words. Your behaviour now should inspire trust and speak to your company values. Create a single place containing your response, any action plans you might put in place, and an FAQ section. Update this consistently if the situation is fluid – and direct people to it whenever needed. This should ideally be an environment you control such as your website – with no sign-up barriers, that is neither limited regionally nor subject to algorithm changes. Be clear about where people can direct their questions and feedback. This can be a dedicated thread in your forum or a designated email account.

Remember what I said about actions and words? Don't just say sorry and move on. This is where you'll put your initial research to the test. Show that you clearly understand where you went wrong and list concrete steps about how you plan to address them. Once you commit to change, it shouldn't remain an empty statement to appease your community. You should work towards it. When you draft your response, say as much as possible but nothing more. Be honest and direct. As the saying goes: *the cover-up is worse than the crime*.

Maybe you're accused of something you did but are convinced there's a justification. If that's the case, state it clearly and transparently. Explain your reasoning, and why you believe it's the best solution for your company, the employees, or the community. Be prepared for pushback and differing opinions – but stick to your decision.

But there's also the option that you're accused of something you did and shouldn't have. This step requires meticulous research about the accusations and, importantly, not talking prematurely. You don't want to first claim you didn't do it, then admit you did but had your reasons – only to be forced to admit that none of this is true. Don't deny it. Sooner or later, someone from the outside will dig deep enough, or someone from the company will spill the beans. Then there's an even more significant trust breach, one you ran into head-first. Avoid this by drafting a direct, honest, and self-reflecting response. What went wrong, why did it happen, and how do you intend to fix it. Don't be unprofessional, and don't direct anger towards individuals. Once everyone working on the crisis communications is satisfied and necessary greenlights have been obtained, publish the message as widely as possible. Then you wait and cross your fingers. Monitor reactions, adjust the course if necessary and support the company by not repeating a similar mistake. Once you believe the issue is fixed and the fire in your community has been extinguished, don't ignore the still-hot embers. The actual community work is only just beginning. People don't forget and forgive immediately, you have to rebuild trust and prove that you meant all those words you put in your statements.

Your company hasn't had any moment of crisis yet? You'll likely get hit sooner or later, and you're lucky to have time to put protections in place should emergencies arise. As a first step, figure out your potential weak spots. What are aspects of your games or company the community might find troubling? Put yourself into an outsider's perspective and look at your company from negative angles. Imagine you heard certain things about your games or company without context or pre-existing sympathies – could anything be perceived as discriminatory, hurtful, or dismissive? I'm not talking about *being* a certain way or *intentionally discriminating*. Online, information will be stripped from its context, and thus, perception is more than enough to cause major issues. In the best-case scenario, you can do this exercise with a group of people to benefit from various points of view. List all possible vulnerabilities and sort them by their likelihood of causing a problem and the level of negative impact. For each risk, write down a few attacks and criticisms you can foresee. Analyse if there's something the company could do. Maybe certain features in the game should be removed, a character needs a rewrite, or an event plan has to be adapted. If there's something you cannot avoid entirely, adjust the communication plans. If you see a risk, try addressing and preventing it instead of hoping it won't become a reality. List bullet points with possible responses for cases you believe cannot be prevented. After doing your due diligence, forward your analysis to the team working on the crisis plan.

Make sure that you know the company's *crisis infrastructure*. Know what to do when you recognise that the canary in your coal mine isn't chirping anymore. Who should you alert? What's the protocol when the worst thing happens? Making good decisions is always easier when you can do the groundwork with a cool head. Of course, you won't be able to change everything. But knowledge can empower you and help you understand even those things you might not yet be able to shape yourself.

7.7.1 The Importance of Good Feedback

There will be times when your colleagues or business partners are responsible for mistakes, as much as you might try to hold yourself accountable. When this happens, it's time for one of the most important skills you can master in your career: giving and receiving proper feedback. If you want to improve as a professional and sharpen your skills, you should be grateful if someone is courageous enough to risk the discomfort of telling you when you messed up. I want to encourage you to be this person for other people. Strive to provide actionable feedback allowing others to work on themselves. So, what does good feedback look like – and why is it relevant?

Let's start with the latter. When done right, feedback improves the individual's behaviour and performance and strengthens the relationship between the giver and receiver. Establishing an honest feedback culture is one of the most important things you can do for a team. It causes everyone to pull in the same direction and learn from each other. Consider who you'd ask for help with an important presentation: the person who always says that everything's perfect from the get-go or the one who will tell you when things don't make sense? Observe some ground rules to avoid being so harsh that no one dares to ask you for your opinion. For one, don't focus your feedback on the person's character. Instead, talk about actions and behaviours. Not only does the person know what you refer to, but more precisely which behaviour you're criticising and what impact this has on others. The icing on the feedback cake would be to recommend how to behave in a similar situation next time. By giving the other person a tangible action and making it about your feelings, the same sentiment makes for more effective feedback.

While we're on feedback, please don't equate it with something inherently negative. Feedback can also be positive and should be shared at least as liberally as the negative type. Show gratitude and appreciation to colleagues, business partners, and community members wherever possible. Not only is it a good habit to get into, but it also pays into the positive atmosphere you want to create in your community and at work.

When others give you feedback, please treat it seriously and don't react defensively, even if it isn't worded particularly constructively. It's essential to learn how to let go of your ego. No one likes hearing that they're not doing something well. But you'll be a better professional (and, dare I say, person) if you learn how to take feedback. Thank the other person for raising the issue. If you don't understand it fully, ask for an example of when and how you behaved that way – don't deflect or defend yourself, and should you feel emotional, take a moment to calm down before you respond. Write the feedback down and collect it in a folder or document. Look at it as rationally as you can. Do you see a grain of truth? Commit to improving yourself and be grateful that the feedback helped you. Is the feedback dismissive? Expecting you to dim your personality? Feel free to ignore it entirely. I aim to listen to all the feedback I get, but I'll still choose what to act on.

7.8 SHARING KNOWLEDGE WITH YOUR COMPANY

Depending on your character, one aspect of this job might sound dull – but it's an integral part of our job to relay the most relevant information to our teams. Furthermore, you'll most likely get asked by your boss to send regular performance reports either way, so the sooner you learn to see their appeal, the less painful it will be. Carve out time in your workweek for reporting. How long you'll spend on it depends on a few things, from the preferences of your lead to the game's status. In a regular week with no major releases, I estimate my personal investment to be 5%. However, in a month where many things happen, this can go up to 25–30% of any given week. No matter how much time you have, set some aside for informing your teammates about important developments, things that happened, and the current health of your community.

7.8.1 Numbers, Facts, and Industry

What topics that you're dealing with might interest the rest of your team? Every CM will probably give you a slightly different answer, but if I had to cluster them, I'd split them as follows:

1. Performance report.
2. Sentiment report.
3. Competitive report/analysis.

Those three fulfil different purposes, and I recommend familiarising yourself with all of them. Let's pick a simple example: you recently released a patch that included bug fixes but also changed a couple of features. The performance report focuses on how many people engaged with the update and related messaging in your community spaces. How many people liked the news or left comments? How many discussion threads were opened on Steam? Are there notable differences between international markets or platforms? You can shine a light on numerous aspects, so pick the ones most important for your company and campaign and present them clearly. However, this doesn't necessarily tell you if people like your update, just that they reacted to it. Here's where the sentiment report comes in.

Instead of looking at the numbers, the sentiment focuses on the *how*. Did people comment because they love or hate it? Is your community sharing the news to mock it? What's the overall mood? I think of these reports as the qualitative part of our research. When presenting your results, be precise and remove your opinions. Don't interpret – yet. If someone writes that they're frustrated because of choppy performance, don't write in the report that it's due to crashes or bugs. At the same time, don't bring harassment or toxicity with you. Remember that part of your job is protecting the developers, and how you present community sentiment is part of this. Don't write down insults or call the game *shit*. It serves no one. It's a balancing act to not misrepresent sentiment but still provide it factually. Sort the elements between positives and negatives, and indicate how common they are. There's a different urgency if three-quarters of your audience report crashes or if it only affects one out of a hundred. Once you have the overview of the reactions, and common comments, include a section in which you interpret the data based on your expertise and recommend how to address the negativity. Be polite. Clearly mark what's from you and what's from the community. Sometimes, you may want to combine performance and sentiment reports after releasing a bigger update.

Finally, there's the competitive report or analysis. You could prepare this well before the update to help decide the campaign approach. Create an overview of selected companies that faced a similar challenge to you – like announcing a potentially unwelcome feature change – and how they communicated it. Include information on how their players reacted, what went well and what could have been improved. If you want to go the extra mile, end the report with custom learnings for your game. How is your player base different, and how could this influence the reaction?

One last piece of advice: always keep the reader in mind. Make it digestible. It doesn't matter if you prepare the most elaborate document about your campaign results if it's so long that no one will read it. Ask yourself some basic questions and use them as guiding principles for all your reports: *what do I want to achieve with this report? What is the shared knowledge base between the readers and me? Who are my readers? Why should they care about my reports? So what?* Think of the needs of your recipients and be ready to answer potential questions. You'll hopefully realise the added value of taking on this extra reporting work.

7.9 COMMUNITY MANAGEMENT IN GAMES JOURNALISM

Marylin Marx

The role of the CM is already diverse in classic video game development. They are helpers, mediators, judges, and managers. That is a lot to manage for just one game. Now imagine being responsible for not just one or a few games, but dozens. That's what it sometimes feels like to be a CM in video game journalism.

WHAT ARE COMMUNITY EDITORS AND WHAT DO THEY DO?

Modern online journalism is no longer just about games, but also about the world around them. Stories and news are told not only by games and their developers, but also by the people who interact with them.

First and foremost, a community editor makes sure that the voices of communities around games are heard. The plural is deliberately chosen because community editors have to deal with a number of games, and therefore numerous communities, all of which function differently.

Especially in times of service games, MMORPGs, and long-lived single-player games, an editor cannot bring the expertise that the community has built up over the years. Due to the nature of their job, they have to keep up with a lot of games in a very short period of time and can usually only work on one or two games in depth over a period of years. They therefore need to contact experts in the community in order to understand complex issues and discussions about said long-lived games.

Depending on the topic and the focus of the publication, community editors need to be able to recognise the feelings and moods of communities that are unfamiliar to them and process their content editorially. What are players saying about the new patch? Why are they angry about a new feature? Which fan creations and mods are being praised to the skies? These are all topics that a community-focused journalist can add to the editorial mix of simple patch news, reviews, or listicles.

Influencers and their topics are also becoming increasingly important in this context, as their opinions and views often carry more weight within the community than those of unknown users. As a result, they often play a decisive role in shaping the communities and are also indispensable for journalistic community content.

HOMEMADE USER-GENERATED CONTENT

But it's not only the games themselves that have created communities. Video game magazines, whether online or in print, are also surrounded by loyal readers who see themselves as part of a community. They have a voice that needs to be heard and opinions that need to be highlighted.

The question "What do our readers think?" is therefore essential for community editors. Content that actively involves your community has several advantages: it offers another perspective on a topic away from editorial opinion, it creates content that cannot be copied by competitors, and it creates an active sense of cohesion in the community. It turns your readers from a passive reader into an active contributor.

Content about and with one's own community usually consists of polls and their results, as well as the prominent embedding of reader quotes in an editorial context and calls to action. Community editors can also go a step further by interviewing experts on individual games from their own community, or even recruiting them to create content. In this way, the relationship between community and editorial can often be more bilateral than is possible in game development.

THE IMPORTANCE OF COMMUNITY MANAGEMENT

Loyal readers not only have opinions about the content of a review, they also feel the need to play an important role in the editorial process. Whether it be ideas and wishes for the written content, or ideals of how a report and its medium should look. They also make an important contribution to quality management. It's the task of the CM team to collect all this feedback, bundle it, and forward it in an evaluated form to the editorial team or the relevant departments (product, layout, sales, etc.).

Just like video games, games journalism has evolved rapidly over the last few years and decades. While print magazines were the main source of information in the early 2000s, websites are now the main source. Their audiences are often divided between loyal, regular readers and new readers reached through Google and the like. There is often tension between these audiences in terms of the content and format of the content offered.

It's in this tension that the role of the CMs is crucial. They are responsible for understanding, processing, and communicating the individual needs of the various members of the very heterogeneous community. At the same time, they act as a voice in both directions. Community editors, in their function as CMs, have to communicate editorial decisions and actions to the community, explain facts, and create understanding for the work of the editorial team. For example, when it comes to finding the right headline.

Depending on the size and capacity of the community, community editors are also responsible for much of the content moderation process, often having to make predictions about which articles might become potential hot topics. Unlike with game developers, a negative review of a game doesn't automatically mean an increase in moderation. In games journalism, it's more often the case that controversial opinions, reviews, or political topics are the content of the articles themselves, and are met with justified or unjustified backlash from their readers.

REQUIREMENTS FOR BECOMING A COMMUNITY EDITOR

If you want to break into the editorial side of community management, you not only need classic community management skills, such as nerves of steel and a good way of expressing yourself, but also a flair for good stories.

In the reality of the job, exciting stories from communities aren't found on their own. They are often hidden in forums and Reddit threads, or only revealed through long or emotional discussions between individual community members. It then takes the instinct of a good editor to turn these stories into a good story for an article.

They also need a thorough knowledge of the games and their communities. Not only do they need to be willing to play the latest and most exciting games, but they also need to immerse themselves in their communities.

Similarly, a community editor needs to take the initiative not just to passively find community stories on social media, but to actively tell them by asking around and asking questions of the in-house community. The more a community editor actively engages with their community, the better stories they will write and the more they will be able to demonstrate how important and, sadly, underrepresented this area of work is.

THE STRUGGLE OF RECOGNITION

The greatest tension in community management is to make one's work visible and to prove that it contributes (monetarily) to the company's goals. While this visibility is already a hurdle for traditional community management in game development, it seems almost insurmountable for community editors.

There is a lack of concrete figures (so-called KPIs) by which success and failure are usually measured. While sentiment analysis is common in game development community management, this is not the case in game journalism, where even a negative text about a game can be positive for coverage. For example, telling the story of a community that is unhappy about a new patch. Or they find topics and community stories that they have not written themselves but pitch to other editors.

All this means that community editors, like CMs in video game development, don't get the recognition and often the budget they need and deserve.

The good news, however, is that with increased political attention within the digital space and initiatives for greater tolerance online, community management and its value are coming into focus. Community storytelling is also becoming more important for newsrooms as people play longer and form communities on Reddit or other social media platforms.

It's now up to us to seize the opportunity and tell not only communities' stories, but also our own.

NOTES

1. Griffiths, Mark, PhD. *Breaking the Stereotype: The Case of Online Gaming.* 2003. https://core.ac.uk/reader/30636768.
2. One of my all-time favourites on the topic is Making Things Happen by Scott Berkun.
3. I have a column titled "Ideas for Later" in my Trello board that I use to organize my work. I put projects in there that don't fit *right now*, and occasionally browse through it to see if I can defrost one of them.
4. Start here: UN. 2023. *Hate Speech.* https://www.un.org/en/hate-speech.

The Importance of Mental Health

8

No job is ever worth ruining your health for. No matter the company, no matter the games, you're what's most important. It's tempting to pour every ounce of energy into it – to prove yourself, show you care, or simply because there's so much to do. But try to internalise that your career shouldn't be a sprint. It should be a marathon. Manage your energy and refill your reservoirs regularly. If you do this openly, you can positively influence the people around you.

8.1 TAKING CARE OF YOURSELF

You cannot pour from an empty cup. You can *try* to pour endlessly, but it'll dry up eventually. Too many people don't prioritise their well-being and fall into the trap of merging with their job into one indecipherable blob of a work-human being. It can be exhilarating – for a while. But then something in the project doesn't go as planned, or you have a personal emergency – suddenly, what was formerly great becomes devastating. You lose contact with friends or family, you start lashing out at co-workers over banalities and don't understand why. You get physically sick. Don't let it get this far.

So much of a CM's work happens on social media, which means it can be especially hard to disconnect. We interact with others and analyse loads of content online, and even when relaxing after hours by watching your favourite creator or scrolling socials, it can quickly turn into hours of responding to messages, comparing marketing materials from other companies, and developing project ideas. Before you know it, it's midnight and you've effectively

DOI: 10.1201/9781003310488-8

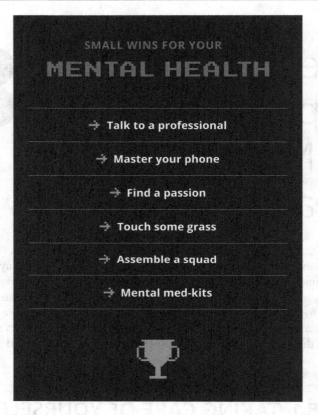

FIGURE 8.1   Steps for protecting your mental health.

not stopped thinking about work. I still sometimes fall into this trap. For some people, work ends after work and they have no problem switching off. Am I a bit jealous? You bet. But I got better because I realised it's essential to carve out time for yourself and be fiercely protective. So, I'll stop beating around the bush: how can you protect your mental health? Figure 8.1 offers some starting points that I'll expand on in this chapter.

8.1.1 Talk to a Professional

First things first, don't take my advice in place of talking to an expert. I strongly advocate for everyone to seek out a therapist at least once in their life. Even if you don't think you need one, a professional can help you discover truths about yourself, become more resilient, and equip you with tools to handle tough situations. If it's hard in your region to access this help, there are great organisations you can contact. Please don't think you must suffer through tough situations alone or that it's somehow part of the package. Asking for help is a true sign of strength.

8.1.2 Master of Your Phone

I don't understand the obsession with overworking yourself. I grew up thinking that once your work is over, getting rest and focusing on life are seen not as a privilege but as the norm. While I know cultural differences apply, I believe everyone should focus more on work-life balance and less on the hamster wheel of productivity. We all know the famous phrase, "Work hard, play hard." Notice how it doesn't say, "Work hard, play hard later once everything's done?"

Especially as a CM, you'll always find work. Another fire to extinguish, feedback to gather, or a message to engage with. Once you add time zones to that mix, you can feel tempted to always be somewhat online – always having one eye on Discord and one on the company Slack. Don't. That kind of behaviour damages your health and the quality of your work. Avoid creating the expectation that you're always on duty. I get that it's incredibly tempting. Initially, I had to trick myself by mastering the biggest culprit – my phone. It's easiest if your employer provides a work phone. Once your daily work ends, turn it off or kill the internet connection in case you need to be available for urgent calls. It gets more complicated when it comes to your personal phone, though. You want to use it in your free time. It's yours, after all. I had to go to extreme lengths to break the habit of accidentally continuing to work from my couch. If this isn't as much of a problem for you, you might not need to do all of this. Which is great!

- It's NO-tification for a reason[1]

  I disabled all work-related notifications on my phone. If I receive an email, I'll see it when I return to work. If someone comments on our social media or something happens on Slack, I only see it if I actively seek out the respective apps. Few things are crucial enough that you must react immediately. For those that are, you can still receive a phone call. Push notifications are evil. Turn them off. In addition, none of my work apps are on my home screen but instead in a separate "work folder." I'm a simple person. If I have to swipe my screen twice, I'll usually forget the app exists until I really need it.

- Don't disturb my mornings

    When I wake up, my phone's *Do Not Disturb* is on. When my alarm rings and I look at my phone, no notifications are urging me to immediately open and react to them. Once I had my breakfast, I'll disable it – unless it's the weekend. There are occasional Sundays where I keep it enabled, and those are nothing but pure bliss. Sorry to all my friends, but it helps me disconnect from work and gives me a couple of hours of inner calm. Similarly, I've enabled the nighttime mode on my phone for the last two hours leading up to my sleep time. Of course, I still use my phone occasionally in bed, but on average, I now read a book – feeling less anxious and sleeping better.

- Tweak Twitter

    Everyone probably has different social media accounts they identify as the main culprit for getting sucked back into work. For some of them, it's effortless for me to just scroll and forget work, so I don't put any limits on those. Pinterest and Tumblr fulfil all my needs for escapism and nonsensical distractions, so all they do is inspire me. However, I found that Twitter enticed me to "just quickly comment," follow games industry drama (of which there's always plenty), or get worked up over something miniscule. Identify which platforms are helping you and which aren't.

    The social media landscape is highly volatile. Changes to platform ownership might mean that certain features won't be available anymore or vanish behind a paywall. Maybe the platform sees a large user migration – that's why I don't believe in specific feature advice about individual platforms. Instead, you can make mindful decisions about what content you see and how you consume it. I'll give you two personal examples.

    Since I still enjoy using Twitter (now technically called X), I found a way to use it without most downsides. There were two main issues for me: (1) I often got outraged when scrolling my feed. (2) I needed to check Twitter for something work-related and then scrolled through the perpetual anger machine for longer than necessary.

    So how did I combat this? First, I created my own wholesome Twitter feeds.[2] I use dedicated and highly curated lists. If you haven't tried it yet, you can pin a list to your feed, allowing you to swipe between thematic feeds depending on your mood and needs. Personally, I have three custom ones: *Updates I really want* made up of only family, friends, and close (former) colleagues, *Gaming CMs* consisting of my industry peers, and *Industry News* with relevant media outlets, selected companies, and their representatives. That way, privately, I can just go through the feed with people of whom I want to see absolutely every update, whereas, for work, the other two lists are self-explanatory and free from distractions.

Instagram is a different beast. Where Twitter caused spontaneous eruptions of anger, Instagram undermined my life satisfaction drip by oversaturated, perfect drip. I know it sounds dramatic, and not everyone reacts the same, but for me, I used to leave the app less happy than when I opened it. To prevent this, I went on a targeted unfollow spree and removed everyone whose postings made me jealous or whose life looked too perfect. Instead, I started following those who use their platform for good, and more artists and musicians. Figure out what works for you. Just remember that you don't have to follow anyone. The platforms should serve you, not the other way around. Especially if you have to spend a lot of time on them, tailor them to your needs and preferences.

I'm aware these things might make me sound like a phone hermit, but protecting my health and time was necessary. The number of games I've played and books I've read in the time I reclaimed are worth it. If you struggle with the feeling that you can never really put down your phone, I encourage you to try some of these.

8.1.3 Find a Passion Not Connected to Your Job

You're likely working or planning to work in the games industry because you love video games. The same is true for me. Because of that, I spend a lot of my free time also watching video game conferences or streams, playing games, visiting events about them, or watching three-hour video essays. Nothing is wrong with that; it keeps me excited about doing my job. However, find at least one thing to be passionate about that's not connected to your work. Ideally, it enriches your overall life and makes it more joyful. On top of that, it might provide new perspectives for your projects because you often get the best ideas when your brain isn't thinking about work at all.

8.1.4 Touch Some Grass

The advice is in the title. Gaming communities sometimes wear it like a badge of honour to not leave the house, lower the curtains, and never see the sun – but please don't do that to yourself. We all know exercise is healthy for the body and mind. I'm not here to make you feel guilty if you're not getting all your daily steps. Even if you just leave the house to sit on a park bench for 30 minutes to listen to music, get some fresh air if possible. If you're physically able to go out into nature (or parks, if you're a city dweller like me), it'll tremendously improve your well-being. That's not an option for you? Surrounding yourself with plants has also been connected to increased calmness and happiness. Use this knowledge and invest in some greenery for your living space.

8.1.5 Assemble A Squad

Friendship is magic. Whether you love surrounding yourself with dozens of people or enjoy the intimacy of two close friends, loneliness is harmful to your health. No matter how busy your life gets, always allocate time in your schedule for your social life. Especially for people like us whose job is so extremely online, it's crucial to cultivate genuine connections, meet people, have phone or video calls, and talk to humans outside of comments.

At the same time, find people within your company to bond with. Having allies to discuss your work life and concerns with is essential. Due to the secretive nature of our business, being close to someone on the inside makes your everyday work life much more enjoyable. Sooner or later, you'll have the urge to share something or simply vent. Just make sure to not fall into a toxic circle of only complaining. There's a delicate balance between occasional ranting and perpetual negativity or gossiping, and the latter two can further decrease your overall happiness and work satisfaction.

8.1.6 Create Mental Med-kits

When our health points are low in a game, we wouldn't hesitate to activate our med-kit, yet for some reason in real life, we expect ourselves to soldier through and just get on with it. Working's not a competition in suffering, and we're allowed to make ourselves feel better when things are extra hard. You alone can judge what's helpful for you and relieves your stress, but here are some things that help me:

- If I feel myself getting angry or annoyed at an email, comment, or Slack message, I do my best not to engage immediately. I'd never recommend ignoring your emotions as I believe they're essential to doing our job well, but you have to channel them and use them wisely. Ride the dragon. So instead, I pace up and down my living room. I prepare tea and stare into space. I blast 2000s emocore from my headphones. The world often looks different if you allow yourself a short break, and I've never regretted taking that time before responding.

- There are days when negativity can take a severe toll on me. For these moments, I keep the big guns: I have a folder in my email inbox and on my laptop where I save kind words, emails with compliments, screenshots of certain achievements or milestones, and community creations or comments. When no amount of tea helps, I open these folders and browse for a few minutes. My day brightens immediately.
- It's almost a cliché at this point, but I constantly feel like an imposter. One day soon, my boss will wake up and realise I'm not performing. Everyone around me works harder and achieves more. When it's that type of day again, I open my trusted Trello board. There I have a column that serves as a visible reminder of everything I've done in the current year and an archive of previous highlights. Instead of deleting a card once the task is done, I move the card to the *What I have done this year* column. That way, I fight back against this toxic trait of second-guessing myself because I see the things I've accomplished at one glance.

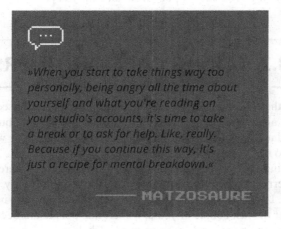

»When you start to take things way too personally, being angry all the time about yourself and what you're reading on your studio's accounts, it's time to take a break or to ask for help. Like, really. Because if you continue this way, it's just a recipe for mental breakdown.«

———— MATZOSAURE

Because self-care is vital for our profession, I've also asked my fellow CMs how they care for their mental well-being. These are the distilled recommendations from more than 40 industry professionals:

- Remove work apps from your personal phone or hide them.
- Disable all phone notifications.
- Only accept friend requests from people you know and enforce personal boundaries.
- Don't share personal news on public channels.
- Speak to a therapist.
- Schedule daily blackout time in your calendar where you don't use the Internet.
- Talk to your colleagues and peers, and ask for help.
- Have hobbies and projects that have nothing to do with your job.
- Get physical exercise.
- Realise there are basically no situations in which everyone is happy.
- Don't use your real name when representing the company.
- Meditate and practice mindfulness.
- Remember that the majority of players only reach out when they encounter an issue.
- Use all your vacation days.
- Spend time with family and friends.

As I've mentioned, these things might not work for you. You might not even recognise yourself in these struggles. We're all affected and soothed by different things. Please think about your little pockets of joy and care for your mental well-being. You cannot pour from an empty cup.

8.2 TAKING CARE OF OTHERS

CMs aren't therapists. Please reread this unless you're a licensed healthcare professional also working in games. It's not only not our job, but it can also be outright dangerous for community members' health and our well-being to attempt to do so.

That being said, it's easy to find yourself in a situation where you're genuinely concerned about your community members. Importantly, this chapter is anecdotal. I don't have the most up-to-date research, and I'm not a sociologist. But over the last couple of years, it's felt like people are becoming more isolated, more on edge, and more in need of help as we've gone from one societal crisis to the next. Many people spend a substantial amount of their social life online, and some have no offline connections. If you connect with community members, you may run into situations where people confess relationship problems to you. I've had people tell me about physical abuse, health issues, deaths in the family, and depression. Some people have even talked to me about ending their life. It's crucial that you set boundaries and don't allow trauma-dumping on you.

At the same time, I fully understand the urge to do *something*. If you have the mental capacity to do so, lend an ear when you can. Sometimes, just talking to someone eases the pain. If you see community regulars becoming more secluded or acting weird, gently reach out. It's a small gesture but can mean the world to someone.

It's up to you to communicate your boundaries and what's acceptable for open discussion. Your community guidelines can also include these elements to prevent triggering conversations. To offer additional support, you can visibly include mental health resources like hotlines in your community spaces. I'll use this chance to blatantly shout out Safe in Our World,[3] a beautiful organisation created by video game professionals to fundraise for mental health charities and increase communication about the topic within our industry. A couple of years ago, I participated in one of their courses dedicated to CMs and mental health. It focused on recognising warning signs in conversations, facilitating people finding help and reaching out to mental health professionals, and what to do in emergencies. I'd strongly recommend checking out their resources and signing up for the training if possible. This isn't sponsored in any way. It was just extremely valuable, and you should learn from proper experts on the topic instead of me.

NOTES

---

1. Sorry.
2. It wasn't my idea – someone I follow shared their journey and how it influenced their happiness. Sadly, I forgot their name but wherever and whoever you are, thank you very much!
3. Visit them here: https://safeinourworld.org/.

Paying It Forward

9

Thank you so much for reading my book! I sincerely hope you took away some helpful information, be it for deciding whether the job is right for you or just getting some new perspectives on the career you're already pursuing. Whatever you learned, I have but one request: please pay it forward. The world is harsh enough. If there's something our industry could always use more of, it's kindness.[1] We're all in this together, and the more senior you become, the more I believe it's your responsibility to help mentor newcomers.

So, if you feel like you know everything this book has to offer, feel free to annotate it and give it to someone you believe could benefit from it. You could even donate it to an educational institution! And if there are things I missed or if you disagree with me on anything, please contact me. I don't think I'll ever be done learning, either – so I hope to hear from you!

Good luck, have fun, and fight the good fight!

NOTE

---

1. And better working conditions across all companies.

DOI: 10.1201/9781003310488-9

References and Reading Recommendations

Brown, Brene. 2017. *Braving the Wilderness.* London, England: Vermilion.

Bacon, Jono. 2019. *People Powered: How Communities Can Supercharge Your Business, Brand, and Teams.* New York, NY: HarperCollins.

Berkun, Scott. 2008. *Making Things Happen. Mastering Project Management.* Sebastopol, CA: O'Reilly.

Community Club. *Salary Repository.* 2023. https://www.community.club/salaries.

Dealessandri, Marie. 2022. "Tips for intentional and healthy networking." GamesIndustry.biz. https://www.gamesindustry.biz/tips-for-intentional-and-healthy-networking-gdc-2022.

Griffiths, Mark. 2003. *Breaking the Stereotype: The Case of Online Gaming.* https://core.ac.uk/reader/30636768.

Hitmarker. 2023. "Career Advice." https://hitmarker.net/career-advice.

IGDA. 2023. "Chapters." International Game Developers Association. https://igda.org/chapters-directory/.

Jones, Carrie Melissa. 2020. *Building Brand Communities. How Organizations Succeed by Creating Belonging.* Oakland, CA: Berrett-Koehler.

Spinks, David. 2021. *The Business of Belonging. How to Make Community Your Competitive Advantage.* Hoboken, NJ: Wiley.

UN. 2023. "Hate Speech" United Nations. https://www.un.org/en/hate-speech.

Printed in the United States
by Baker & Taylor Publisher Services

Printed in the United States
by Baker & Taylor Publisher Services